Anonymus

# Catalogue of the Smith Cabinet

Part Second

Anonymus

**Catalogue of the Smith Cabinet**
*Part Second*

ISBN/EAN: 9783742802262

Manufactured in Europe, USA, Canada, Australia, Japa

Cover: Foto ©Thomas Meinert / pixelio.de

Manufactured and distributed by brebook publishing software
(www.brebook.com)

Anonymus

# Catalogue of the Smith Cabinet

# CATALOGUE

—OF—

# THE ✦ SMITH ✦ CABINET,

## [PART SECOND.]

Comprising a large and varied assortment of American and Foreign Gold,
Silver, Copper, Bronze and Nickel Coins, Medals, &c., also, Ancient
Greek and Roman Gold, Silver and Bronze Coins and
Medals; Paper Money, Numismatic Books,
and a large assortment of Store Cards,
Politicals in Silver and Copper,
Personals, &c., &c.

Included in the two sales will be found the U. S. Silver Dollars of
1794, 1836, 1838, 1839, 1851, 1852 and '58.

ALL THE RARE U. S. HALF DOLLARS; ALL BUT TWO OF THE
U. S. QUARTERS; ALL THE U. S. DIMES; ALL THE U. S.
HALF DIMES; MANY FINE AND UNCIRCULATED U S
CENTS, HALF CENTS, AND A LARGE VARIETY OF AMER-
ICAN COLONIAL COINS.

*A portion of the above will be offered at each days Sale.*

# BANGS & CO., Auctioneers,

## 739 & 741 BROADWAY, NEW YORK.

*Tuesday, Wednesday and Thursday, October 19, 20, 21, 1880.*

Commencing each Day at 2.30 P. M.

# Catalogued by MASON & CO.

## 143 NORTH TENTH STREET, PHILADELPHIA.

☞The Auctioneers will execute any Bids entrusted to them.☜

PRESS OF
EDWARD HIRSCH & CO., 30 South Fourth St.
PHILADELPHIA.

# EXPLANATORY.

The owner of the Smith Cabinet, fearing that a six days continuous coin sale would prove tedious and otherwise inconvenient to many buyers, concluded to divide his extensive collection, and make at proper intervals two sales of three days each ; and in adopting this plan, we would state, that our object has been to give as varied a character to each sale as possible ; hence we have selected for each day a good portion of the choice pieces in each series to interlard the great quantity and variety of those pieces not generally so highly valued. In pursuing the above course, we have sacrificed, in a measure, system to convenience. A package of catalogues of Part 1 & 2, has been sent to each Coin Dealer in the U. S. and Canada, and a large number of single copies mailed to collectors, whose names are upon our books to date. In case any dealer should require a further supply of catalogues, or if any omissions have occured, immediate notice to the undersigned will supply the deficiency. All coins, medals, &c., in both sales, are guaranteed genuine, unless otherwise described. Attention is solicited to the grand opportunity, afforded by the two sales, to secure bargains among the lots offered in various portions of the catalogue. Collectors of foreign silver and copper coins, medals, &c., will find much of interest under these headings, while collectors of Business Cards, Politicals, American Medals, &c., will find a rich field to help out their series. The rare and fine American pieces in the catalogues speak for themselves, and a number will command unusual attention for rarity and condition.

MASON & CO.,

143 North Tenth Street,

September, 1880.                                        PHILADELPHIA.

# CATALOGUE.

## MISCELLANEOUS FOREIGN COINS.
### MEDALETS, &C.

1  Iron Cross, 50th year, Jubilee at Leipsic, 1863 rev. "16-19 Oct. 1813" very fine, rare, size 28 by 26.
2  1818 Geo III Half Crown, brass, fine.
3  1771 " " Rev. Arms, patterns, farthing size, brass, fine, scarce, 2 pieces.
4  1771 Same, varieties, good, 2 pieces.
5  Thick English brass piece, resembles a weight marked "36 Shillings," poor, size 15.
6  English Drug Weights 1 and 2 drachms, brass, fine 2 pieces.
7  1730 Obverse, Goblet, "*Signum Senatori*". Reverse. Arms, (Cologne,) silver, copper centre, size 13.
8  Jewish Shekel, white Metal, copy, good, size 22.
9  Same, Struck copy in brass, proof, scarce.
10  Japanese ¼ Bou, gold (value $1 00,) fine.
11  1848 Model Half Farthing, Victoria, good rare.
12  1593 Henry IV. Early French coin, fair, rare.
13  Admiral Vernon medals, large and small, copper, very poor, 2 pieces.
14  1814 "Un Decime" (Napoleon) reverse, large N. thick, good, scarce.
15  1874 Straits Settlements, 1 Cent, copper, uncirculated, scarce.
16  German Singing Soc'y Medalet, Goddess of Lib. "N. Y. Jul, '71." brass, very fine, size 16.
17  1869 Jamaica Penny, nickel, fine, scarce.
18  1870 Same, Half Penny, good, scarce.
19  1871 Same, Penny and Half Penny, fine, scarce, 2 pieces.
20  1869 20 Kopek, Russia, silver, fine.
21  1870 Medal, "Put On The Whole Armor Of God," w. metal, very fine, size 20.
22  1801 Peace Medalet G. Britain and France, brass, fair, scarce.
23  English coins and medalets, various, copper and brass, large and small, fair to fine, 10 pieces.
24  French and German coins, Medalets and Jetons, fair to uncirculated, large and small, brass, &c., 18 pieces.

## MISCELLANEOUS AMERICAN COINS, MEDALS, MEDALETS, TOKENS, &c.

25  1803 Kettle ½ and ¼ Eagle, brass, gilt, good, 2 pieces scarce.

26  1860 U. S. Gold Dollar, struck in silver, pierced, good, scarce.

27  Kossuth Medalet, brass, fine, scarce, size 18.

28  1860 Abolition Medalet, Success to Rep'n Principles, brass, proof, size 15.

29  Stephen Girard, Lovett's Card, copper, proof, size 20.

30  Beck's Public Baths, Richmond, reverse, nude female bathing, copper, fine, rare, size 18.

31  1800 Silver Token, obverse, table, wine and bread. Legend, "This do in remembrance of me," reverse, burning bush, "*Nec Tamen Consumebatus.*" On periphery is the inscription, "Presbyterian Church of Charleston, S. C. 1800," fine, very rare, size 18.

32  1861–5 W. Va. Medal, obverse, Fame crowning a Soldier, eagle, wheat, arms, &c., Rev. reads, "Presented by the State of W. Virginia," copper, good, rare. size 24.

33  Bust of Maj. Gen'l Hooker, reverse, U. S. Army, &c., copper, fine, size 20, scarce.

34  Sunday School medal, oval, obverse, Saviour, reverse, Bible, bronze proof size 24 by 16.

35  Holmes, Booth and Hayden's card; inscription, "This is nickle silver," &c., reverse, blank, fine, scarce, size 16.

36  1875 "Battle of Bunker Hill," June 17, '75, reverse, Monument, copper, pierced, good, scarce, size 18.

37  1847 Herr Alexander, (N. Y.), thick, copper, gilt, fine, size 18.

38  Bust of Harrison, reverse, Log Cabin, copper, fine, size 18

39  1860 Bust of Lincoln, reverse, "Free Homes," copper, good, size 18.

40  Yates & Co., Card, Phila., brass, fine, 3 pieces.

41  1867 Kleinstuber's Card, 318 State Street, Milwaukee, white metal, very fine, size 16.

42  Thos. Depuy, 37 S. Second Street, Phila., w. metal, good, size 15.

43  Patapsco Co's Card, Baltimore, w. metal, very fine. size 14.

44  1866 Price Bro's. Baltimore, nickel card, fine, size 18.

45  Richardson's Umbrella Card, 229 Broadway, N. Y., brass, very fine, size 15.

46  Gilmore's Coliseum Card, Boston, brass, very fine, 2 pieces, size 18.

47 Key's & Diehl's Card, Phila., brass, very fine, size 15.
48 1864 J. A. Bolen, reverse, Liberty Cap, thick, copper, very fine, scarce, size 18.
" 49 1864 U. S. 2 cent, bronze piece, struck on a 1 cent planchet, fair, rare.
/ 50 Cards, Tokens, Medalets, Politicals, &c., fair to fine, brass, copper and w. metal, 13 pieces.
51 Shell Cards, size of Dollar and Half Dollar, varieties, brass, fine, 9 pieces.

## AMERICAN COLONIAL COINS.
### (CONTINUED FROM LAST SALE.)

(Catalogued by Crosby's Work on Colonials.)

### VERMONT.

52 1785 Cent. Reverse, Immune Columbia, fair, better than usually found in sales, rare.
53 1785 Cent. Vermonts Res Publica. Good, black, scarce.
54 1786 " Vermontensium. 9 Trees, good.
55 1786 " Auctori Vermon. Baby head, fair.
56 1787 " Vermon Auctori. 2—A. Very good.
57 1787 " " Britannia. 1—C. Good, scarce.
58 1788 " " " 1—A. Fair, "
59 1788 " " " 2—A. Good, "
60 1788 " " " 3—B. Small planchet, fair, rare.
61 1788 Cent. Vermon Britannia. 3—B. Large planchet, good.
62 1788 Cent. Vermon Britannia. 4—C. Fair.
63 1788 Tory Cent, Georgius III Reverse. Inde et Lib. fair, scarce.
64 1788 Cent. "I. K." cut on the head, scarce.

### CONNECTICUT.

65 1785 Cent. 4—F. Very good.
66 1785 " 4—F. Negro head, poor.
67 1786 " 2—A. Et lib inde, fair.
68 1786 " 2—D. Inde et lib, good.
69 1787 " 1—C. Mutton head, good.
70 1787 " 4—L. Horned Bust, fine.
71 1787 " 6—P. Laughing head, fine.
72 1787 " 9—E. A scarce combination, good.
73 1787 " 12—Q. Misstruck, otherwise good.
74 1787 " 14—II. Good, but cleaned bright.

75  1787  Cent.  33—S.  Fine.
76  1787   "    33—Z.  Very good.
77  1787   "    37—E  Very good.
78  1787   "    36—L.  Good.
79  1787   "    43—Y.  Counfe., fair.
80  1788   "    2—D*.  Very fair.
81  1788   "    5—B.  Good, scarce.
82  1788   "    11—G.  Very good, scarce.
83  1788   "    16—N.  Good, scarce.

## NEW JERSEY.

84  1786  Cent.  2—E.  Fine, light olive.
85  1786   "    3—E.  Good.
86  1786   "    4—C.  Fair.
87  1786   "    4—H.  Horse without ears, crooked date.
         good, scarce.
88  1786  Cent.  4—H.  Without bridle, good.
89  1786   "    4—H.  Different from either, good, but
         brightened.
90  1787  Cent.  1—B.  Large knobs, very good, scarce
         variety.
91  1787  Cent.  1—B.  Small knobs, good.
92  1787   "    3—F.  A rare combination, good.
93  1787   "    4—D.  A rare variety, good.
94  1787   "    5—E.  Fine, weak impression.
95  1787   "    5—E.  Fair, interesting, scarce.
96  1787   "    7—I.  Large planchet, fine.
97  1787   "    8—K.  Pluribs, very fair, scarce.
98  1787   "    9—I.  Large planchet, very good.
99  1788   "    4—C.  Very good.
100 1788   "    5—D.  Head left, very poor.
101 1788   "    5—D.    "    "    "    "

## NOVA CONSTELLATIOS.

102  1783  Nova Constellatio, Roman letters, blunt rays,
        very good.
103  1783  Nova Constellatio, Roman letters, sharp rays,
        very fine, rare.
104  1783  Nova Constellatio, Roman letters, smaller, fine,
        dark.
105  1783  Nova Constellatio, Roman letters, duplicate, fine.
106  1785  Nova Constellatio, blunt rays, good.
107  1785  Nova Constellatio, sharp rays, very good.

## SILVER COINS OF SPAIN.

108 1708, '10, '12 Charles III, 2 Reals, (25 cts. each,) good, 3 pieces.
109 1717, '21, '22 Same, varieties, fair to good, 4 pieces.
110 1734 Philip V, 1 and 2 Reals, good, 2 pieces.
111 1736 Same, 2 Reals, fair.
112 1747, '9 Same, (Pillar) varieties, fair, 2 pieces.
113 1761 Charles III, 2 Reals, fair.
114 1761 Same, 1 and 2 Reals, fair to good, 2 pieces.
115 1769, '71 Same, 2 Reals, varieties, good, 2 pieces.
116 1775 Same, 4 Reals, good.
117 1777   "   2 Reals, fair.
118 1777   "   8 Reals, ($1.00,) good.
119 1780   "   1 Real, good.
120 1781   "   8 Reals,   "
121 1782   "   2   "   "
122 1782   "   4   "   "
123 1788   "   4   "   "
124 1791, '2 Charles IV, 2 Reals, varieties, poor, 2 pieces.
125 1792 Same, 4 Reals, good.
126 1793   "   "   "   "
127 1795   "   8   "   "
128 1795   "   4   "   "
129 1797   "   8   "   "
130 1797, '9, 1802 Same, 2 Reals, varieties, fair, 3 pieces.
131 1810 Ferdinand VII, 8 Reals, good.
132 1810 Same, variety.
133 1810, '11, '12 Joseph Napoleon, (Pistareens,) (20 cts. each,) good, varieties, scarce, 3 pieces.
134 1814 Ferdinand VII, 8 Reals, good.
135 1814 Same, 8 Reals, variety, pierced, good.
136 1816 Same, 8 Reals, good.
137 1819   "   8   "   "
138 1821   "   8   "   fine.
139 1821   "   4   "   variety, good.
140 1830   "   2   "   "   fine.
141 1837 Isabel II, 2 Reals, fine.
142 1857 '66, Same, 2   "   good, 2 pieces.
143 1876 Alfonso XII, 2 Reals, very fine.
144 1737 to 1810; 1 Real, varieties, poor to good, 15 pieces.
145 1721 to 1850; 1 Real, poor to good, 9 pieces.
146 1739 to 1804; Small Spanish Coins, varieties, poor to good, 16 pieces.
147 1871 Amadeo I, Spain, 8 Real, good.

# SILVER COINS OF AUSTRIA AND GERMANY.

148  1610 Rix Thaler, Austria, fine, rare.
149  1645 Crown of Frederick Wm. of Prussia, very fine, very rare.
150  1665 Crown of Brunswick, fine, rare.
151  1692 Frederick III, ⅔ of a crown, good. scarce. rare.
152  1693 Same, very good, rare.
153  1696 Same, fine, rare.
154  1707 Crown of Josephus of Austria, very fine, proof surface, very rare.
155  1764 Thaler of Frederick, good.
156  1765 Same, very good.
157  1767 Thaler, Mar. Theresa, good.
158  1772 Rix Thaler, Bavaria, good.
159  1775 Same, good.
160  1785 Russian Thaler, Frederick, very fair.
161  1786 Same, very good.
162  1789 Same, Frederick Wm., good.
163  1790 Same, fine.
164  1792 1 Thaler, Leopold II, very good.
165  1794 Same, variety on reverse, good.
166  1797 Crown Thaler of Austria, pierced. good.
167  1810 Crown Thaler of Bavaria, good.
168  1825 Francis I, Austria, Rix Thaler, very good.
169  1840 Fred. Wm. III, Prussia, 2 Thaler piece, very good.
170  1841 Fred. Wm. IV, Prussia, same, fine.
171  1841 Ludwig I, 2 Thaler piece, uncirculated.
172  1841   "   II, same, very fine.
173  1842 Fred. Wm. IV, Prussia, 2 Thalers, fine.
174  1844 Ludwig II, 2 Thalers, very good.
175  1845   "   I, 2 Gulden, fine
176  1846 Fred. Wm. IV. Prussia, 2 Thalers, fine.
177  1850 Same, fine.
178  1851 Maximilian II, 2 Gulden, very fine.
179  1854 Same, 2 Thalers, very good.
180  1861 Johann V, Saxony, 2 Thalers, very fine
181  Frederic I, Wurtemberg, Rix Thaler, date scratched out otherwise good.

# MISCELLANEOUS FOREIGN SILVER COINS.

## PORTUGAL, BRAZIL, PERU, &c.

182  1810  960 Reis, ($1.00,) good.
183  1812  Same, fine.
184  1813  "  uncirculated,
185  1814  "  fine.
186  1817  "  variety, very good.
187  1825  Rep. of Peru, 8 Reals, fine.
188  1832  Same, good.
189  1833  "  "
190  1835  "  "
191  1838  "  uncirculated.
192  1838  "  4 Reals, fine.
193  1842  "  8  "  good.
194  1844  "  4  "  base, poor.
195  1864  1 Sol, ($1.00,) good.
196  1865  Same, very good.
197  1868  "  "  "
198  1869  "  uncirculated.
199  1870  "  "
200  1871  "  "
201  1872  "  "
202  1873  "  "
203  1874  "  "

## SILVER COINS OF TURKEY, &c.

204  20 Piastres (90 cts) uncirculated.
205  Same, very good.
206  Medal, Crimea, size of 20 Piastres, good.
207  5 Piastres, very fine.
208  Same, variety, very fine.
209  2 Piastres, fine.
210  1  "  good.
211  Small coins, varieties, good, 3 pieces.
212  Very small coins, good, 2 pieces.
213  10 Piastres, early coin, base, good.
214  Same, smaller, thin coin, base, good, 4 pieces.
215  Lot of small thin coins, copper and base metal, fair to fine, 21 pieces.
216  Large and small coins, silvered, very fine, 4 pieces.

## EAST INDIA SILVER COINS.

217 1 Rupee, (45 cts) engrailed edge, fine.
218 Same, variety, good.
219 " plain edge, good.
220 " variety, good.
221 ½ Rupee, hammered edge, fine.
222 Same, good.
223 ¼ Rupee, uncirculated, scarce.
224 1835 1 Rupee, Wm. III (E. India Co..) varieties, good.
    2 pieces.
225 1840 Same, Victoria, uncirculated, scarce.
226 1862 " fine.
227 1876 " uncirculated.
228 1840 '1 Same, ½ Rupee and 2 Annas, fine, 2 pieces.
229 Complete Set Victoria 1875, 1 Rupee; ½ Rupee; ¼ Rupee;
    2 Annas; uncirculated, with description on native pa-
    per, scarce, 4 pieces.
230 1862 Same, 2 Annas, fine.
231 1874 " ¼ Anna and ½ Anna, copper, uncirculated,
    2 pieces.

## SILVER COINS OF BURMAH.

232 1 Rupee (Peacock) very good.
233 Same, ½ Rupee " "
234 " ¼ Rupee, fine.
235 " 2 Annas, "
236 " Set (Peacock) good, 4 pieces.
237 " 2 Annas, good, 2 pieces.
238 " ¼ Anna, (Peacock) copper, good, 2 pieces.
239 " fair, 3 pieces.
240 " poor, 3 pieces.

## COPPER COINS OF GREECE.

241 1838 Set, 10, 5 and 2 Lepta, reverse, Arms, very fine,
    3 pieces.
242 1839 Same, 2 Lepta, very fine.
243 1842 and 52, Two Lepta, good, 2 pieces.
244 1848 Same, thick, 10 Lepta, good.
245 1849 " fine.
246 1851 " 10 and 5 Lepta, fine, 2 pieces.
247 1851 '8, '9, Two Lepta, good, to uncirculated, 3 pieces.
248 1869 Bust, 10, 5, 2 and 1 Lepta, set, good to fine,
    4 pieces.
249 1870 Same, 10 Lepta, uncirculated.

# UNITED STATES DIMES.

'250 1796 Cracked die, obverse fine, reverse very fine, an excellent specimen of this rare coin.
' 251 1797 13 stars, very good, both obverse and reverse, nearly fine, extremely rare.
252 1797 Same, good, excepting date, which shows '97 only.
253 1798 over '97 Fine, might be termed uncirculated, rare.
254 1798 Perfect date, cracked die, in same condition as last, rare.
255 1800 All plain, very good, extremely rare.
256 1801 Good, rare.
257 1802 Very good, rare.
258 1803 Good, rare.
259 1804 A very beautiful specimen, very fine, excessively rare, without a scratch, and only slightest mark of circulation.
260 1805 Good, scarce.
261 1807 Very fine, planchet a little uneven, scarce.
262 1809 Fine, scarce.
263 1811 Very fine, very scarce.
264 1811 over 1809 Very good, rare.
265 1814 Large date, fine.
266 1814 Small date, good.
267 1820 Small wide date, very fine.
268 1820 Large close date, fine.
269 1820 Large O in date; good.
270 1821 Small date, fine.
271 1821 Large date, very good.
272 1822 Very good, very rare.
273 1823 Fine.
274 1824 over 23, good.
275 1824 over 22, good.
276 1825 Good.
277 1827 Very fine.
278 1828 Large date, good.
279 1828 Small "      "
280 1829 Uncirculated.
281 1830      "
282 1831      "
283 1832 Very good.
284 1833 Very fine.
285 1834 Good.
286 1835 Uncirculated.
287 1836      "

| | | | |
|---|---|---|---|
| 288 | 1837 | Fine. | |
| 289 | 1837 | Without stars, fine. | |
| 290 | 1838 | " " O. Mint, good. | |
| 291 | 1838 | Uncirculated, scarce. | |
| 292 | 1839 | " | |
| 293 | 1840 | Fine. | |
| 294 | 1841 | Dull proof, rare. | |
| 295 | 1842 | Very fine. | |
| 296 | 1843 | " " | |
| 297 | 1844 | Good. | |
| 298 | 1845 | Dull proof, rare. | |
| 299 | 1846 | Fine, rare. | |
| 300 | 1847 | Uncirculated. | |
| 301 | 1848 | " | |
| 302 | 1849 | " | |
| 303 | 1850 | A lump of silver from the die, resembling a bird on left shoulder of Goddess, a rare curiosity, we term it the "Dove variety," very fine. | |
| 304 | 1851 | Fine. | |
| 305 | 1852 | Dull proof, rare. | |
| 306 | 1853 | No arrows, fine. | |
| 307 | 1853 | Arrows, uncirculated. | |
| 308 | 1854 | Uncirculated. | |
| 309 | 1855 | " | |
| 310 | 1856 | Small date, O. Mint, uncirculated. | |
| 311 | 1856 | Large date, fine. | |
| 312 | 1857 | Uncirculated. | |
| 313 | 1858 | " | |
| 314 | 1859 | O Mint, proof. | |
| 315 | 1860 | Very fine. | |
| 316 | 1861 | " " | |
| 317 | 1862 | " " | |
| 318 | 1864 | Good. | |
| 319 | 1865 | Fine. | |
| 320 | 1866 | Good. | |
| 321 | 1867 | Proof. | |
| 322 | 1868 | Uncirculated. | |
| 323 | 1869 | Fine. | |
| 324 | 1870 | Dull proof. | |
| 325 | 1871 | Very fine. | |
| 326 | 1872 | Uncirculated. | |
| 327 | 1873 | No arrows, very fine. | |
| 328 | 1873 | Arrows, uncirculated. | |
| 329 | 1874 | Uncirculated. | |
| 330 | 1875 | " | |

" 331   1876  Uncirculated.
  332   1877      "
  333   1878  Proof.
' 334   1879  Uncirculated.

## SILVER COINS OF GERMANY.

' 335   1795  24 Grosch. (45 cts) Brunswick, fair, pierced.
' 336   1814  Thaler (66 cts) Prussia, good.
' 337   1818  Same, fine.
' 338   1818     "   variety, good.
  339   1825  Fred. Wm. III, Prussia, Thaler (66 cts.) fine.
'' 340   1830  Same, good.
'' 341   1831     "   uncirculated.
' 342   1840     "   variety, fine.
' 343   1841     "   reverse, Arms crowned, good.
'' 344   1855     "   head right, fine.
'' 345   1855     "   head left, very fine.
'' 346   1866     "   reverse, eagle crowned, uncirculated.
'' 347   1867  Thaler of Saxony, (65 c.) good.
'' 348   1867  Same, Arms crowned, uncirculated.
'' 349   1868     "   eagle crowned, uncirculated.
'' 350   1869     "   fine.           .
'' 351   1869     "   good.
'' 352   1870     "      "
'' 353   1871     "   uncirculated.
'' 354   1871  "Sieges Thaler." Prussia, King Wm., reverse, fe-
             male seated, crowned, uncirculated, scarce.
/ '' 355   1871  Saxon Thaler, reverse, equestrian figure, uncircu-
             lated, scarce.
/'' 356   1871  Thaler, Ludwig II, reverse, female seated, uncircu-
             lated, scarce.
'' 357   1871  Saxon Thaler, reverse, Arms, fine.
/'' 358   1874  Ludwig II, 5 Mark piece, proof, scarce.
'' 359   1876  King Wm. Prussia, 2 Mark piece, uncirculated.

## SILVER COINS OF ITALY.

/' 360   1809  Five Lire, Napoleon, good, scarce.
'' 361   1812  Same, pierced, good, scarce.
'' 362   1826     "   Chas. Felix, fine, scarce.
/'' 363   1848  5 Lire, Reverse, Republic of Venice, good, rare.
'/ 364   1869  "   "   Victor Emanuel II, fine.
'' 365   1870  Same, good.
/' 366   1874     "   uncirculated.

367 1810 2 Lire, Napoleon, fair, scarce.
368 1863 " " Victor Emanuel II, good.
369 1867 " " 1 Lire, 10 & 5 Soldi, Pius IX, fine 4 pieces.
370 1808 1 " Napoleon, poor.
371 1811 Same, fair.
372 1827 Same, Chas Felix, 1 Lire, fine.
373 1863 " Victor Emanuel II, good.
374 1863 " varieties, fine, 2 pieces.
375 1867 " fine.
376 1808 15 Soldi, Napoleon, good, scarce.
377 1808 10 " " " "
378 1810 5 " " " "
379 1811 Same, good, Scarce.
380 1814 " " "
381 1815 10 Soldi, Maria Louise, Parma, good, scarce.
382 1826 Same, Chas. Felix, 50 Centesimi, fine.
383 1829 '30 Same. 25 Centesimi, good, 2 pieces.
384 1847 Chas Albert, 50 Centesimi, fine.
385 1860 Victor Emanuel, 50 Centesimi, fine.
386 1863 " " 50 and 20 Centesimi, fine, 2 pieces.
387 1866, '8, Pius IX, 10 Soldi, fine, 2 pieces.
388 1867 Victor Emanuel, 50 Centesimi, uncirculated.

# SILVER COINS OF FRANCE.

389 1811 5 Franc, Napoleon, very fair, scarce.
390 1811 Same, 2 Franc, good, scarce,
391 1814 " good, scarce.
392 1816 5 Franc. Louis XVII, good.
393 1823 Same, good.
394 1824 " "
395 1826 " Charles X, good.
396 1828 1 Franc, same, uncirculated, proof surface.
397 1831 5 " Louis Philipp, good.
398 1833 2 " same. good.
399 1834 5 " " very good.
400 1835 '7, 1 and 2 Franc, good, 2 pieces.
401 1840 5 Franc, same, good.
402 1845 Same, good.
403 1847 1 Franc, same, good.
404 1849 2 Franc, Republic, good.
405 1866 2 and 1 Franc, Empire Napoleon III, uncirculated, 2 pieces.
406 1867 Same, uncirculated, 2 pieces.
407 1868 " fine, 2 pieces.

408 1869 1 Franc, same, fine.
409 1871 2 " Republic, fine.
410 1872 1 " same, uncirculated.
411 1875 5 " "Liberty, Equality, Fraternity," fine, scarce
412 1828 1 Franc, Charles X, good, scarce.
413 1851 1 Franc, Republic, fine.
414 1852 1 " Louis, Napoleon, good.
415 1858 '9, 1 Franc, Empire, good, 2 pieces.
416 1872 1 Franc, Republic, fine.
417 1811 ½ " Napoleon, fair, rare.
418 1812 Same, fair, rare.
419 1828 '30; ½ Franc of Chas X, good, 2 pieces.
420 1833, '4, '8, '9, '46, '7, '8, ½ Franc, Louis Philipp, varie-
    ties, fair to good, 7 pieces.
421 1850 '1, ½ Franc, Republic, good, 2 pieces.
422 1858 '9, '62, '4, '5, '6, '7; 50 Centimes, good, to very fine,
    10 pieces.
423 1829 '30, ¼ Franc, Chas. X, good, 2 pieces.
424 1833, '4, '5, '7, '40, '1, '2, '3, '4, '5, '6, Louis Philipp,
    ¼ Franc and 25 Centimes, fair to fine, 11 pieces.
425 1849, '50, 20 Centimes, Republic, good, 2 pieces.
426 1857 Same, uncirculated.
427 1858, '9, '60, '7, 20 Centimes, Empire, fine, 5 pieces.

# U. S. COPPER CENTS.

428 1793 Chain, fair, rare.
429 1793 Wreath, vine and bars, small "Liberty," twig at
    right angles, very good, rare.
430 1793 Liberty Cap, fair, rare.
431 1794 Die cracked through centre, fine.
432 1795 Thick lettered edge, good, scarce.
433 1795 Medium Planchet, good.
434 1795 Thin Planchet, fine, rough.
435 1796 Liberty Cap, very good.
436 1796 Fillet, good.
437 1797 Plain edge, fine, rough.
438 1797 Indented edge, good.
439 1798 over '97, good.
440 1798 Plain border, fine, dark.
441 1798 Milled border, fine, dark.
442 1798 Broad date, good.
443 1799 Good, black, rare.
444 1800 over '99 fine, dark.
445 1800 Perfect date, large Planchet, good.

| | | |
|---|---|---|
| 446 | 1800 | Small Planchet, fine, dark. |
| 447 | 1801 | $\frac{1}{100}$, fine, dark. |
| 448 | 1801 | $\frac{0}{100}$, fine, black. |
| 449 | 1801 | $\frac{1}{100}$ over $\frac{0}{00}$ fine, dark olive. |
| 450 | 1802 | $\frac{1}{100}$, fine, dark. |
| 451 | 1802 | $\frac{0}{100}$, Good. |
| 452 | 1803 | $\frac{1}{100}$, fine, dark olive. |
| 453 | 1804 | Cracked Die, good, little weak at date, rare. |
| 454 | 1805 | Very fine, has nick on edge, dark. |
| 455 | 1806 | Fine and sharp, dark even surface. |
| 456 | 1807 | over '6, fine, dark, Liberty, weakly struck. |
| 457 | 1807 | Perfect date, large $\frac{1}{100}$, very good. |
| 458 | 1807 | "   " small $\frac{1}{100}$ "   " |
| 459 | 1808 | 13 Stars, good, dark. |
| 460 | 1808 | 12 "   "   " scarce. |
| 461 | 1809 | Good, dark, scarce. |
| 462 | 1810 | over '9, very good. |
| 463 | 1810 | Large close date, fine. |
| 464 | 1810 | Broad small date, very good. |
| 465 | 1811 | over '10, good, black. |
| 466 | 1811 | Perfect date, fine, stars weak, scarce. |
| 467 | 1812 | Fine, corroded. |
| 468 | 1813 | Good. |
| 469 | 1814 | Crossed 4, fine, corroded. |
| 470 | 1814 | Plain 4, fine, dark. |
| 471 | 1815 | altered from '45, g od. |
| 472 | 1816 | Perfect Die, fine. |
| 473 | 1816 | Broken die, fine. |
| 474 | 1817 | Date left of bust, 17 close, very fine, light olive. |
| 475 | 1817 | Date under bust, 17 apart, fine, dark. |
| 476 | 1817 | Close date, under bust, cracked die, good. |
| 477 | 1817 | 15 stars, fine, scarce. |
| 478 | 1818 | Uncirculated, varnished. |
| 479 | 1819 | over '18, Large date, uncirculated, light olive, |
| 480 | 1819 | Small broad date, no Mint Mark, fine. |
| 481 | 1819 | " close " Mint Mark, fine. |
| 482 | 1820 | " date, very fine, steel color. |
| 483 | 1820 | Large " fine, light olive. |
| 484 | 1820 | "   " connected stars, very fine, light olive. |
| 485 | 1821 | Good, scarce. |
| 486 | 1822 | " |
| 487 | 1823 | over '22, Perfect date, good. |
| 488 | 1823 | Perfect date, good. |
| 489 | 1824 | over '23, Good, scarce. |
| 490 | 1824 | Perfect date, good. |

491 1825 Fine.
492 1826 Very fine and sharp, bright, varnished.
493 1827 Fine, light olive.
494 1827 Broken die, good.
495 1828 Close date, light olive.
496 1828 Broad " good.
497 1829 Fine.
498 1830 Double border, close date, very good.
499 1830 Broad date, fine, dark.
500 1831 Very fine, light olive.
501 1831 Connected stars, fine, light olive.
502 1832 Fine, black.
503 1833 Fine, dark olive.
504 1834 " light "
505 1834 Connected stars, fine, dark olive.
506 1834 Double profile, very good.
507 1835 No Mint Mark, fine, light olive.
508 1835 Mint Mark, very good,
509 1836 " " " " dark olive.
510 1836 No Mint Mark, very good, light olive.
511 1836 Broken die, fine, dark olive.
512 1837 Fine, dark olive.
513 1838 Uncirculated, shows portion of red.
514 1839 Erratic die, over date, resembles 1830, good, rare.
515 1839 Head of '38, very fine, dull stars.
516 1839 "Silly Head," very good.
517 1839 "Booby Head," very fine, light olive.
518 1839, '40 Head, uncirculated, partly red.
519 1840 Large date, very fine, light olive.
520 1840 Small " fine, dark olive.
521 1841 Fine.
522 1842 Large date, fine.
523 1842 Small " " black.
524 1843 Date left of bust; reverse, small letters, fine, scarce.
525 1843 Date under bust; reverse, large letters, very good.
526 1844 Very fine, light olive.
527 1845 " " steel color.
528 1846 Small crooked 6, uncirculated, dull stars.
529 1846 Large straight 6, good.
530 1847 Fine.
531 1848 Uncirculated, partly red.
532 1849 Very fine, dull stars.
533 1850 Uncirculated, red.
534 1851 Same.
535 1852 "

536   1853 Uncirculated, light olive.
537   1854 Same, dull stars.
538   1855 Same, straight date.
539   1855 Same, slanting   "
540   1856   "    uncirculated, red.
541   1857 Large date, uncirculated, straw color.
542   1857 Small   "   uncirculated, dull stars.

# SILVER COINS AND TOKENS; GREAT BRITAIN, &C.

543   1561 Elizabeth Shilling, good, scarce.
544   1562 Same, variety, good.
545   1567   "   pierced, poor.
546   1591   "   good.
547   1608 Charles II, shilling, fair, scarce.
548   1696 William III,   "   good,   "
549   1696 Sixpence, good, scarce.
550   1697 Same, shilling, good, scarce.
551   1711 Queen Ann Shilling, good, scarce.
552   1712   "   "   "   fine.
553   1723 George, Shilling, good.
554   1745   "   II   "   very good.
555   1757 Same, Sixpence, good.
556   1758   "   fine.
557   1787 George III, Shilling, very fine.
558   1787   "   "   Sixpence, uncirculated.
559   1805   "   "   Tenpence, Irish, good, scarce.
560   1806 Same, Five pence, fair, scarce.
561   1811 George III, 1s., 6d. Bank Token, good, scarce.
562   1811 "One Shilling Silver Token," reverse, John Small-
      page, Leeds, fine, rare.
563   1812 Manchester Shilling Token, A Bank, &c., fine, rare.
564   1816 George III, Shilling, fine,
565   1816 Same, poor, 2 pieces.
566   1817 George III, Half Crown, good, scarce.
567   1819 Same, good,
568   1821 "George IIII," Crown, St. George and Dragon,
      unworn but bruised.
569   1822 George IV, Anchor Shilling and Sixpence, good,
      2 pieces.
570   1824 George IV, Shilling and Sixpence, uncirculated,
      2 pieces.
571   1826 George IV, Lion Shilling, very fine.

572  1826 Same, good.
573  1834 William IIII, Shilling and Sixpence, fine, 2 pieces
574  1838 Victoria Shilling and Sixpence, fine, scarce, 2 pieces.
575  1839 Same, Shilling, fine.
576  1840 Same, Sixpence, dull proof.
577  1841 Same, Shilling, good.
578  1872 Same, 1 Florin, uncirculated.
579  1875 Same, Sixpence.

## MAUNDAY MONEY, &C.

580  1676 Charles II, 3 pence, good, rare.
581  1680 Same, 2 pence, pierced, good, rare.
582  1687 James II, 3 Pence, very good, scarce.
583  1689 Wm. and Mary 4 Pence, fine, rare.
584  1706 Anna, 4 Pence, fine, scarce.
585  1758 George II, Penny, fine, scarce.
586  1762    "   III, 3 Pence,  "       "
587  1776    "   III, 1 and 2 Pence, very fine, 2 pieces.
588  1800    "   III, 4 Pence, good.
589         "   III, Victoria, &c., 4 Pence, varieties, good, 5 pieces.
590         Same, 3 Pence, varieties, fine, 4 pieces.
591  1838 Same, 1½ and 2 Pence, good to fine, 10 pieces.

## MISCELLANEOUS COINS, &C.

592  Germany, England, Spain, Italy, &c., large and small coins, forming a collection, mostly base, some in silver, poor to fine, 55 pieces.
593  Another lot, same, 65 pieces.
594    "      "      "    52 pieces.
595    "      "    but few silver pieces, poor to good condition, 132 pieces.

## UNITED STATES HALF CENTS

596  1793 Very good, nearly fine, good color, liberty pole distant from lower part of bust, large close date, rare.
597  1793 Another, same condition, pole nearly touches lower part of bust, broad small date, rare.
598  1794 Bust high up on planchet, broad date, very fine, good color.
599  1794 Bust in centre of planchet, fine, good color.
600  1795 Thick Die, lettered edge, fine, scarce.
601  1795 Thin   "   fine, date a little weak.

602   1796 Black and somewhat corroded. Every letter and figure of obverse distinct, reverse, fair, better than usually offered at coin sales (cost owner $30.) extremely rare.

603   1797 Fine, black, slightly corroded.

604   1800 Fine, dark olive.

605   1802 Very good, better than usually offered, rare.

606   1803 Fine, dark olive.

607   1804 Plain 4, fine, light olive, no tie to wreath.

608   1804 With tie to wreath. Broken Die, crossed 4, fine, light olive.

609   1805 Plain 5 distant from bust, no tie to wreath, fine, light olive.

610   1805 Five touches bust, tie to wreath, very good.

611   1806 Uncirculated, red.

612   1807 Fine, black.

613   1808 Fine, good color.

614   1809 Very fine, dark olive.

615   1810 Uncirculated, partly red.

616   1811 Broken die, very fine, light olive, rare.

617   1811 Fine, dark, rare.

618   1825 Fine, proof surface.

619   1826 Uncirculated, red.

620   1828 13 stars, uncirculated, red.

621   1828 12 stars, fine, light olive.

622   1829 Fine.

623   1831 Solid copper electrotype, uncirculated, red.

    (This and the rare dates that follow, are not the common lead electrotypes,) rare.

624   1832 Uncirculated, light olive.

625   1833    "      "     "

626   1834     "       red.

627   1835     "       "

628   1836 Solid copper electrotype, uncirculated, red, rare.

629   1840 Same.

630   1841   "

631   1842   "

632   1843   "

633   1844   "

634   1845   "

635   1846   "

636   1847   "

637   1848   "

638   1849   "    Small date.

639   1849 Large date, Uncirculated, light olive.

640  1850 Uncirculated, light olive.
641  1851 Uncirculated, light olive.
642  1852 Solid copper electrotype, uncirculated, red, rare.
643  1853 Uncirculated, light olive.
644  1854     "          "       "
645  1855     "       red.
646  1856     "       "   rare in this condition.
647  1856 Another, uncirculated, partly red.
648  1857 Uncirculated, red.

## ANCIENT GOLD COINS.

649  Greek of Cyrene, Siephium, Gold Value $2.50, fine, rare,
     size 8.
650  Solidus of Justinian, Gold Value $3. Very fine, scarce,
     size 14.
651  Solidus of Justinus and Sophia, (Gold Value $3.) Good,
     scarce, size 9.
652  Morocco. Year 1235 of Hegira (Gold Value 2.50) Good,
     size 11, rare.
653  Japanese ¼ Bou, rectangular (Value $1.) fine.
654  Small Turkish coin (Value $1.) very fine.

## AMERICAN SILVER MEDALS,
## MEDALETS, &C.,

655  Bust of James Madison "President of the U. S. A. D.
     1809," reverse, clasped hands, tomahawk and pipe,
     motto, "Peace and Friendship." From an Indian Chief
     in the West, (silver value about $3.50) good, pierced,
     rare, size 32.
656  Battle of "The Five Forks." Medal made from a U. S.
     silver dollar. Obverse, five solid gold three pronged
     forks, arranged in the form of a star, in the centre of
     which is engraved: "Devins, 1st Div. Carried the
     Five Forks. A. LINCOLN." Between the points of
     the stars is engraved "Sheridan's—Cavalry—Co. D.
     Cal. Bat.—Co. F. 2d Mass.—Cav. Res. Brig." En-
     grailed border or rim, reverse nearly blank showing a
     few stars from the dollar, very fine, possibly unique.
657  1864 Bust of Lincoln, reverse, "A. LINCOLN, An Honest
     Man," &c., medalet, fine, size 12.
658  1865 Obverse and reverse, busts of Lincoln and Grant,
     no inscriptions, medalet, size 12.

659   Bust of Grant, beneath which is an Indian, pipe, and twig of laurel, Legend, "U. S. of America." "Liberty, Justice and Equality. Motto, *Let Us Have Peace.*" Around the border, a wreath of leaves, separated by four shields; reverse, globe, bible and agricultural implements. Motto, "*On Earth Peace Good Will Toward Men* 1871." Around the border, 36 stars. Proof, pierced, silver ring attached, (value in silver about $5) rare, size 40

660   Independence Hall, reverse, The Liberty Bell, 1776—1876, medalet, pierced, ring attached, size 12.

## MISCELLANEOUS COINS, &C.

661   Large copper coin of Siam. Pagoda &c., very fine, scarce.

662   Ancient medal. Bust of Francis Quirinus, reverse, an animal and 2 male figures, "Perpetna Sobolls," very fine, slightly touched with verdigris, bronze, rare, size 23.

663   1689 James II Gun Money, (XXX March) very fine, scarce, size 20.

664   1689 Same, (XII Dec.) fine, scarce, size 17.

665   1689 Same, (XXX Aug.) good, scarce, size 18.

666   1689 Same, (XII Jan.) good, scarce, size 16.

667   African "Link Money," shape of letter G, round, $\frac{3}{4}$ of an inch in diameter, copper, weighs about $\frac{1}{2}$ pound, rare. (There is one of these curious pieces in the U. S. Mint, Phila.) about $2\frac{1}{2}$ inches in diameter.

668   1659 Saxon silver Crown fished up by oystermen in Raritan Sound, N. J. fair, considerably oxodized, fair.

669   1659 Another, much thinner found at the same place.

670   Bust of Edward VI. Shilling, very good, rare.

671   Jewish Shekel; obverse, very fine, reverse, fair, very thick, silver, size 14.

672   Half Shekel or Bekah, silver, thick, good condition, size 12.

    (Note.—Certificates and letters from Robert Morris, L. L. D. La Grange, Ky. accompany the lots 671 and 672 stating that these pieces are genuine, and were exhumed in 1876 at Caesarea in Palestine and vouched for as authentic by Rolla Floyd, Esq. of Joppa. These guarantees are offered with the coins, cost owner $40.)

673   Coin of Germanius Caesar, 1st bronze, good.

674   Coin of Constantinus Pius, reverse, a galley, steered by a winged Victory, 2d brass, good, (Certificates from **Dr. Morris accompany lots 673 and 674.**)

675 Widow's Mite, good, scarce, (Certificate of Dr. Morris accompanies this piece.)

676 Tetradrachm, (B. C. 600) reverse, a bull. An early forgery, description accompanies it.

677 Thin silver plated coin of Edward the Confessor, very fine, not guaranteed, size 13.

678 Small bronze Roman Coins exhumed at Pompeii, poor, 6 pieces.

679 1690 Crown of James II, obverse, equestrian figure, copper, very fine, rare.

680 Wax and plaster casts of Roman Intaglios, good, interesting, 4 pieces.

681 1794 Three Gl. German Coin, struck in brass, good.

682 1696 Silver Maunday Money, William, reverse, thistle, 4 pence, fair, rare.

683 1641, '65, 72 Rude lumps of copper used as coins, countermarked, poor, 3 pieces.

684 East India Coins, small, thick, copper, good, 3 pieces.

685 1679 Charles II, silver, 2 and 3 pence, pierced, good, 2 pieces

686 1837 "Half Cent worth of Pure Copper, U. S. Standard," copper, fine, scarce.

687 Large Russian Coins, copper, good, scarce, 2 pieces.

688 Bust of David Hossack, M. D., U. S. Mint medal, bronze, silvered, fine, size 21.

689 Copper coin, Repub. of Paraguay, good, scarce.

690 1870 Medal "Put On The Whole Armor of God," copper, fine, size 20.

691 Sage's copper Token, No. 6, State House, Phila., very fine, size 20.

692 1778 Same, Lieut. Col's Commission, signed by Pat. Henry, cleaned, a little torn, very rare.

693 1782 Commonwealth of Virginia, Colonel's Commission, Militia, (Martin Pickett,) signed Benj. Harrison and Wm. Davies, good, rare.

694 Japanese bank bill, ($1.00,) torn.

695 Brazil Note, 1000 Reis, (below par,) good.

696 1852 Kossuth Note, $50.00, Hungarian Fund, signed L. Kossuth, new and clean, scarce.

697 Blue Ticket of Diplomatic Corps, admit to Inauguration of Hayes, clean, scarce.

698 Same, white, "Admit bearer to Senate Gallery," clean, scarce.

699 Red Ticket of admission, Electoral Commission, No. 152, clean, rare.

700 1877 Same, yellow, "Counting vote for President and Vice President," clean, signed by Ferry and Sam. Randall, scarce.

## SECOND DAY'S SALE.

### CONFEDERATE PAPER MONEY, &c.

701 1863, '4 One Dollar Notes, Richmond, good, 50 pieces.
702 1863, '4 Same, variety in shades, &c., 50 pieces.
703 1864 Five Dollar Notes, Richmond, clean, 8 pieces.
704 1864 Ten " " " " 50 pieces.
705 1864 Twenty " " " " 50 pieces.
706 1864 Fifty " " " " 50 pieces.
707 1864 One Hundred Dollar Notes, Richmond, clean, 45 pieces.
708 1862 One Hundred Dollar Notes, Negroes in field, clean, rare, 2 pieces.
709 1862 One Hundred Dollar Notes, Train of cars, clean, scarce. 6 pieces.
710 1862 One Hundred. Va. Treasury Note, clean, scarce.
711 1861 Sept. 2, Fifty Dollars, torn, rare.
712 1852 $1.00, Hungarian Fund, L. Kossuth, clean, rare.

### FOREIGN SILVER MEDALS.

713 1597 Male figure surrounded by shields, containing Arms of various principalities of Germany, reverse, "*Ricct. Faciendo Neminem Timeas*," good, size 26.
714 Mexican medal with loop, obverse, Virgin Mary, reverse a Cross, &c., 1786, fine, size 22.
715 1713 Obverse, bust of Queen Ann of England, reverse, figure of Britannia, shipping, guns, &c., struck from a private die, fine, very rare, size 22.
716 1732 Obverse, Saviour, Virgin, Cross, &c., reverse, people kneeling, (German,) fine, size 20.
717 1742 May 17, obverse, battle, "*Victoria A. D. Chottusitz*" reverse, memorial monument, flags, guns, &c., surmounted by a male bust, "*Victori Perpetuo*," good, size 21.
718 1751 French Medalet, obverse, a Jester, Cornucopia, &c., "*Fortunae Reduci*," reverse, 2 busts, "M. Therres," fine, size 16.

719    1779 Pole surrounded with vine and grapes, reverse, rocks, male figure, tree, &c., (German,) fine, size 20.

720    1810 Obverse, Cathedral, reverse, in two lines, "Napoleon Maria—Louise," very fine, size 21.

721    1815 Obverse, an angel, above it Wellington, below it, Waterloo, reverse, bust of George III, steel ring attached. Edge reads "John Palmer, 10th Royal Reg't. Hussars," fine, rare, size 23.

722    1815 Blucher and Wellington, reverse, German inscription, (Alliance medal,) dull proof, rare, size 23.

723    1817 German medalet, pulpit, bible, &c., reverse, Evangelical Jubilee, fine, size 14.

724    1821 Obverse, Sun, reverse, Liberator of Peru, very fine, size 24.

725    1828 "Ludwig I," reverse, monument, very fine, size 24

726    1833 Obverse, male and female figures, cornucopia, &c., reverse, King Wm., Wurtemberg, fine, size 25.

727    1848 Bust of Christian VIII, of Denmark, reverse, Fred. VII, King of Denmark, fine, size 24.

728    1859 Obverse, equestrian figure on monument, reverse, bust of Emperor of Russia, fine, pierced, size 23

729    1865 Bust of George V, Hanover, reverse, siege of Waterloo, good, size 20.

730    1865 Arms of Bremen, reverse, Singing Society, &c., proof, rare, size 21.

731    1871 Same, Freedom Thaler, proof, rare, size 21.

732    1872 Arms of Hanover, reverse, female figure, shield, &c., proof, rare, size 21.

733    1872 Busts of John and Amelia, King and Consort of Saxony, reverse, 1822, 10 of Nov. 1872, very fine, size 26.

734    Busts of Melgarejo and Nunoz of Bolivia, good, size 16.

735    Bust of Louis XV, reverse, throne, 1830, good, pierced, size 19.

736    Lot of coins, medalets, &c., English, French, German, S. American, &c., fair to good, 13 pieces

737    Lot of Silver and Base metal English, German, Italian, and Turkish Coins, large and small, fair to good, 9 pieces.

738    Spanish Half Dollar of 1793, reverse covered with fine lathe work, script letters, &c.

## UNITED STATES HALF DIMES.

739    1794 Very good, date excellent, rare.

740    1795 Cracked die, very good, scarce.

741 1796 Uncirculated, slight pin mark on left field, very rare.
742 1797 Very fine, very rare.
743 1800 Uncirculated.
744 1801 Fine, slightly scratched on obverse.
745 1802 Good specimen in date, bust, word Liberty and stars. Very little worn but weak in stars on left of bust, and slightly indented, reverse, not quite as good as obverse. Guaranteed original, cost owner $77.50—of the highest rarity in any condition.
746 1803 Fine, rare, a really desirable piece.
747 1805 Nearly, if not quite, uncirculated; slightest mark of friction on cheek of Liberty. Next in rarity to the 1802, and in this condition excessively rare, (cost $50.)
748 1829 Uncirculated, peculiar sharp edge.
749 1830 Uncirculated.
750 1831     "         proof surface.
751 1832     "         "       "
752 1833 Proof, rare.
753 1834     "      "
754 1835     "      "
755 1836 Very good.
756 1837 Uncirculated.
757 1837 No stars, Liberty seated, uncirculated.
758 1838  "    "   O Mint, good, rare.
759 1838 Uncirculated, proof surface, scarce.
760 1839 Very fine.
761 1840 Uncirculated, proof surface, rare.
762 1841 Fine.
763 1842 Very fine.
764 1843   "      "
765 1844 Fine.
766 1845   "
767 1846 Very good, rare.
768 1847 Uncirculated, proof surface.
769 1848 Small date, fine.
770 1848 Large date, very good.
771 1849 Proof.
772 1850 Fine.
773 1851 O. Mint, fine.
774 1852 Uncirculated.
775 1853 No arrows, proof.
776 1853 Arrows,       "
777 1854 Proof.
778 1855 Fine.

779 1856 Fine.
780 1857 "
781 1858 Uncirculated.
782 1859 Proof.
783 1860 Fine.
784 1861 "
785 1862 Uncirculated.
786 1863 Fine.
787 1864 Uncirculated.
788 1865 Proof.
789 1866 Very fine.
790 1867 " "
791 1868 Fine.
792 1869 Uncirculated.
793 1870 "
794 1871 "
795 1872 "
796 1873 "

## FOREIGN COPPER COINS.

797 Netherland of India, 2½ cent 1857, fine.
798 1834 to 40 Same, 2 cent pieces, good, 5 pieces.
799 1830 to 40 " 1 " " fine, 3 pieces.
800 1836 Same, ¼ Stiver, uncirculated.
801 1825 '6 Same, ¼ Stivers, good 3 pieces.
802 1805 to 22 Batavia, ¼ good, 4 pieces.
803 1857, '8, '9 Same, One cent and ½ cent, fine, 2 pieces.
804 1858, '9 Same, ½ cent, 2 pieces.
805 1810, '30 India, ¼ Anna, varieties, fine, 2 pieces.
806 1858, '62 Same, varieties, good, 2 pieces.
807 1791, '8 " ¼ Anna (scales) good, 2 pieces.
808 1832, '3 " (scales) good, 2 pieces.
809 1804 E. India Co., large and small coins, fine, 2 pieces.
810 1835 Same, ¼ Anna, uncirculated, 2 pieces.
811 1845, '53 Same, ½ cent, varieties fine, 2 pieces.
812 1831, '5 " ½ Anna, (scales) fine, 2 pieces.
813 1845 Same, ¼ cent, fine.
814 1848, '62 Same, ½ Anna, uncirculated, 2 pieces.
815 1835 Same, Half Anna, thick, fine.
816 1845 " 1 cent, very fine.
817 1863, '8 Russia, 3 and 2 Kopek, fine, 2 pieces, scarce.
818 1823 One Kopek, fine.
819 1863, '5 Hong Kong, 1 cent, fine, 2 pieces.
820 1866 Same, uncirculated, 2 pieces.
821 1865, '75 Same, very fine, 2 pieces.

## AMERICAN BRONZE MEDALS, &C.

822  1776 July 4, "Libertas Americana," very fine, proof surface, original, very rare, size 30.

823  Marriage Medal, bust of Robert and Louise Gilmore, "Married 50 years. Sept. 25, 1821," proof, rare, size 26.

824  Lafayette, "The Defender," &c., good, original, scarce, size 30.

825  Franklin and Montyon, proof scarce, size 27.

826  Adam Eckfeldt, Chief Coiner U. S. Mint, 1839, proof, rare, size 34.

827  David Hosack, M. D., proof, size 21.

828  McClellan; reverse, wreath, thin, proof, size 22.

829  Same, very thick, proof.

830  "  reverse, "First in the Hearts of His Soldiers," fine, pierced, size 20.

831  1863 Jan. 1, Lincoln, reverse, medal series of the U. S. Mint, proof, scarce, size 29.

832  U. S. Grant, Pacific R. R. medal series of U. S. Mint, very fine, size 29.

833  Same, "15th Amendment," proof, size 18.

834  1874 Maryland Institute, obverse, Justice, ships, &c., reverse, "Awarded for Handcarts," Baltimore, fine, size 32.

835  Lovett's Medalet, Penn's Treaty, very fine, size 20.

836  Sage's Medalet, Bust of Chas. I. Bushnell, Numismatic Gallery No. 1, very fine, size 20.

837  Same, Henry Borgort No. 2, very fine.

838  "  Frank Jandon No. 6,  "  "

839  Sage's historical medalet, British Prison No. 1, very fine.

840  Same, City Hall N. Y. No. 2, very fine.

841  "  Old Sugar House N. Y. No. 2, very fine.

842  "  Paul Morphy No. 3, very fine.

843  Shell in bronze of the "Great Seal," of the C. S. A., Feb. 22, 1862.  Rare and very fine, size 56.

## FOREIGN SILVER COINS.

844  Spain, "Cob" money, (value 25c) fair.

845  "  "  "  "  20c  "

846  "  "  "  "  12½c  "

847  "  "  "  "  "  "

848  "  "  "  "  5c. to 10c. each, fair, 5 pieces.

849 1610 Spain, Small rude coin, good, rare.
850 1687 Germany, Small, rude coin, fair, rare.
851 1611 Italy, Small, rude coin, pierced, poor, rare.
852 1598 " " " " fair, rare.
853 1793 Germany, 5 Mark piece, pierced, good.
854 1762 Portugal, "4 Macutas," (20 cts.) good, 2 pieces.
855 Spain, Pistareens, poor, 3 pieces.
856 1794 Belgium, Crown, good, scarce.
857 1749 " "X St." (25c.) good, scarce.
858 1802 Portugal, 320 Reis, good, scarce.
859 1791 Belgium, "1 G." (50c.) good scarce.
860 1816 Norway and Sweden, ½ Specie dollar, fine.
861 1855 Same, 24 Skillings, fine.
862 1845-53 " " " fair to good, 3 pieces.
863 1875 Same, 1 Krona, fine.
864 1871 " 15 Skilling or 50 Ore, uncirculated.
865 1845-7-54 Same, 12 Skillings, good to fine, 3 pieces.
866 1855-6-8-71 Same, 25 Ore, good to fine, 4 pieces.
867 1855-7-64-5-74 Same, 10 Ore, good to fine, 6 pieces.
868 1872 Same, ½ Specie dollar, good.
869 1848-52-55 Same, ½ Specie dollar, good to fine, 3 pieces
870 1838 Fred. VI, ½ Specie dollar, uncirculated, scarce.
871 1856 Same, ½ Rix Dollar, good.
872 1857 Fred. VII, 16 Skilling, very fine.
873 1868 Austria, Francis Joseph, 2 Florin, ($1.00), uncirculated.
874 1865 Same, M. Theresa, ½ Rix dollar, (45 cts.) good.
875 1829 Greece, 4 Drachma, (72 cts.) uncirculated.
876 1873 " 2 " good.
877 1873 " 1 " uncirculated.
878 1833 " ½ " "
879 1874 " 50 Lepta, fine.
880 1873-4 " 1 and 2 Drachma, 50 and 20 Lepta, uncirculated, set of 4 pieces.
881 1827 Russia, 25 Kopeks, good, scarce.
882 1855 Same, fine.
883 1854 " 20 Kopeks, Fine.
884 1869 " 20 and 15 Kopeks, uncirculated, 2 pieces.
885 1869 " 20 Kopeks, very fine,
886 1875 " 15 " fine.
887 1845 " 10 " proof, pierced.
888 1855-63-67 Same, 10 Kopeks, fine, 3 pieces.
889 1864-69 " "15 Remna," good, 2 pieces.
890 1872 Same, 25 Remna, uncirculated.
891 1836 " 5 Kopeks, good.

892   1840-56 Wurtemberg, ½ Gulden, good. 2 pieces.
893   1845 Bavaria, ½ Gulden, good.
894   1848 Netherlands, ½ Gilder, good.
895   1705 Sweden, 4 Groshen, obverse, man and tree, fine, rare.
896   1864 Netherlands, 1 Gulden, uncirculated.
897   1854       "       ¼    "        "
898   1859 Bremen, 12 Grote, very fine, 2 pieces.
899   1858 Austria, ¼ Florin, good.
900   1859 Same, uncirculated.
901   1866 Belgium, 1 Franc, fine.
902   1872 Prussia, three 2½ and one ½ Silver Groshen, base, uncirculated, 4 pieces,
902½  1871 Same, 1 silver Groshen, base, uncirculated, 3 pieces
903   1873 Germany, 1 Mark, uncirculated.
904   1874 Same, proof.
905   1874   "    fine.
906   1875   "    proof.
907   1875   "    proof.
908   1875   "    uncirculated.
909   1859 Denmark, Danish West Indies, 10 and 20 cts., (Ship,) fine, 2 pieces.
910   1862 Same, 20 and 10 cts., very fine, 2 pieces.
911   1760 Poland, 1 Florin, obverse, bust of the king, reverse, arms, good.
912   1813-15 Switzerland, 5 Batz, fair, 2 pieces.
913   1850 Same, Helvetia, 2 Francs, fine.
914   1850   "     1 Franc, fine.
915   1874   "     2    "      "
916   1850-1 "     1 and two ½ Franc, good, 3 pieces.
917   1873 Belgium, 5 Francs, fine.
918   1868   "      2   "   good.
919   1867   "      1   "   fine.
920   1858 Canada, 20 cts., fine.
921   1865   "      5 and 20 cts., good, 2 pieces.
922   1870   "      50 and 25 cts., uncirculated, 2 pieces.
923   1870   "      10 and 5 cts., good, 2 pieces.
924   1872 Same, 50 and 25 cts, very fine, 2 pieces.
925   1873-1-6 Same, two 10 cts. and two 5 cts. good to fine, 4 pieces.
926   1824 Rio de La Plata, 2 Reals, (20 cts.) good.
927   1826 Same, fair to fine, 2 pieces.
928   1861-5 Guatemala, 2 Reals, (25 cts. each) variety, good, 2 pieces.
929   1824-30 Central America, 1 Real, good, 2 pieces.

—

930    1848 Same, ½ Real, counter-marked by a die, rev. a lion, etc., good, rare.

931    1829-30-3 Republic of Columbia, 1 Real, fair to good, 3 pieces.

932    1844 Republic of Chili, 1 Real, good.

933    1624 One Groshen, very thin coin, fine, rare.

934    1708 4 Mariengroshen, good, scarce.

935    1845 Bremen, 12 Grote, good.

936    1866-8 Belgium, 50 Centimes and 20 Centimes, fair to good, 4 pieces.

937    1849-56-63-69-71 Ten cts. Netherlands, fine, 5 pieces.

938    1850-63 Same, 5 cts, fine. 3 pieces.

939    1853 Hanover, 12 Einen Thaler, uncirculated,

940    1874-5 Germany, 50 and 20 Pfenning, uncirculated, 2 pieces.

941    1875-6 Same, uncirculated, 2 pieces.

942    1837-49-69 Austria 20 and 10 Pfenning, uncirculated, 3 pieces.

943    1838, '44 France, 1 Franc, two ½ Francs and ¼ Franc, fair to good, 4 pieces.

944    1864 Austria, 1 Markka (20 cts.) proof.

945    Small coins of India, various, good. 3 pieces.

946    "   "   " Germany, good to fine. 3 pieces.

947    1867, '9, '71 Germany, 3 and 1 Kreutzer, base, uncirculated, 3 pieces.

948    1876 Venezuela, 1 Centavo, nickel, fine.

949    Germany, large base coins, good to fine, 10 pieces.

950    Same, Small base coins, good to uncirculated, 7 pieces.

## UNITED STATES CENTS.

951    1793 Vine and Bars, twig has a base line, small letters, good, rare.

952    1793 Chain, poor, rare

953    1794 Fallen 4, nearly fine.

954    1795 Thin planchet, 1 cent high in wreath, nearly fine.

955    1795 Medium planchet, very good.

956    1796 "Liberty" variety, poor, rare.

957    1796 Liberty Cap, good, black.

958    1797 Good, black.

959    1798 over '97 Good.

960    1798 Perfect date, nearly fine.

961    1799 over '98 Fair, rare.

962    1800 over 1799, Very good,

963 1800 Large planchet, good.
964 1800 Small " "
965 1801 $\frac{1}{100}$, good.
966 1801 $\frac{1}{000}$, "
967 1801 $\frac{1}{000}$, broken die, good.
968 1801 $\frac{1}{100}$ over $\frac{1}{000}$. fine.
969 1802 Very small $\frac{1}{100}$, fine.
970 1802 Large broad $\frac{1}{100}$, fine, black.
971 1803 " $\frac{1}{100}$, black, fine.
972 1803 Small $\frac{1}{100}$, good.
973 1804 Fair, rare.
974 1805 Fine, black.
975 1806 Nearly Fine, dark.
976 1807 over '6 Very good.
977 1807 Perfect die, good.
978 1807 Broken Die, good.
979 1808 Good.
980 1808 12 stars, good, scarce.
981 1809 Good, scarce.
982 1810 over 9 good, black.
983 1810 Nearly fine.
984 1811 over 10, good.
985 1811 Perfect date, good.
986 1812 nearly fine.
987 1813 Good.
988 1814 Crossed 4, nearly fine.
989 1814 Plain 4, good.
990 1815 Altered from '45, good.
991 1816 Double headed cent, soldered.
992 1816 Good.
993 1817 Date under bust, fine.
994 1817 " to left of bust, good.
995 1817 Broad date, good.
996 1817 Close date, cracked Die, good.
997 1817 15 stars, very good, scarce.
998 1818 Good.
999 1818 Cracked Die, good.
1000 1819 Large date, fine.
1001 1819 Small " "
1002 1820 Small O, fine, black.
1003 1820 Large O, Fine.
1004 1821 Good, scarce.
1005 1822 nearly Fine, black.
1006 1823 Good, scarce,
1007 1824 over 23, good.

| | | |
|---|---|---|
| 1008 | 1824 | Perfect date, good. |
| 1009 | 1825 | Nearly Fine. |
| 1010 | 1826 | Fine, black. |
| 1011 | 1827 | Good. |
| 1012 | 1827 | Broken die, good. |
| 1013 | 1828 | Nearly fine. |
| 1014 | 1829 | " " |
| 1015 | 1830 | Good. |
| 1016 | 1830 | Broken die, good. |
| 1017 | 1831 | Nearly fine. |
| 1018 | 1831 | Connected stars, nearly fine. |
| 1019 | 1832 | Nearly fine. |
| 1020 | 1833 | " " |
| 1021 | 1834 | " " |
| 1022 | 1835 | Good. |
| 1023 | 1836 | " |
| 1024 | 1837 | Fine. |
| 1025 | 1837 | Cracked die, fine. |
| 1026 | 1838 | Very fine. |
| 1027 | 1839 | '38 Head, nearly fine. |
| 1028 | 1839 | Silly Head, good. |
| 1029 | 1839 | Booby Head, Cracked die, fine. |
| 1030 | 1839 | '40 Head, fine. |
| 1031 | 1840 | Nearly fine. |
| 1032 | 1841 | " " |
| 1033 | 1842 | Large date, fine. |
| 1034 | 1842 | Small " " |
| 1035 | 1843 | Date left of bust, fine. |
| 1036 | 1843 | " under " nearly fine. |
| 1037 | 1844 | Nearly fine. |
| 1038 | 1845 | Fine. |
| 1039 | 1846 | Large 6, good. |
| 1040 | 1847 | Fine. |
| 1041 | 1848 | " |
| 1042 | 1849 | " |
| 1043 | 1850 | Very fine. |
| 1044 | 1851 | Uncirculated, red. |
| 1045 | 1852 | " light olive. |
| 1046 | 1853 | " partly red. |
| 1047 | 1854 | Very fine. |
| 1048 | 1855 | Straight date, uncirculated, partly red. |
| 1049 | 1855 | Slanting " fine. |
| 1050 | 1856 | Uncirculated, partly red. |
| 1051 | 1857 | Large date, fine. |
| 1052 | 1857 | Small date, good. |

## UNITED STATES HALF CENTS.

| | | |
|---|---|---|
| 1053 | 1793 | Very good, light color, rare. |
| 1054 | 1794 | Thick Planchet, fine. |
| 1055 | 1794 | Thinner Planchet, small date, black. |
| 1056 | 1794 | Large date, good. |
| 1057 | 1795 | Thick Planchet, lettered edge, very good, scarce. |
| 1058 | 1795 | Thin " nearly fine. |
| 1059 | 1797 | Fine, very black. |
| 1060 | 1800 | Fine, scarce. |
| 1061 | 1802 | Good, rare. |
| 1062 | 1803 | Nearly fine. |
| 1063 | 1804 | Crossed 4, very fine. |
| 1064 | 1804 | Plain 4, very fine. |
| 1065 | 1805 | Fine. |
| 1066 | 1806 | Uncirculated, red. |
| 1067 | 1807 | Good. |
| 1068 | 1808 | Very fine. |
| 1069 | 1809 | Uncirculated. |
| 1070 | 1810 | Very fine. |
| 1071 | 1811 | Close date, very fine. |
| 1072 | 1811 | Broad date, light color, very fine. |
| 1073 | 1811 | Broken die, black, fine. |
| 1074 | 1825 | Very fine. |
| 1075 | 1826 | " " |
| 1076 | 1828 | Uncirculated, light olive. |
| 1077 | 1829 | Nearly fine. |
| 1078 | 1831 | Altered from '34, poor. |
| 1079 | 1832 | Fine. |
| 1080 | 1833 | Uncirculated, light olive. |
| 1081 | 1834 | " " " |
| 1082 | 1835 | " " " |
| 1083 | 1849 | Fine. |
| 1084 | 1850 | " |
| 1085 | 1851 | " |
| 1086 | 1853 | " |
| 1087 | 1854 | Very fine. |
| 1088 | 1855 | " " |
| 1089 | 1856 | " " partly red. |
| 1090 | 1857 | Uncirculated, red. |

## SILVER COINS OF CHINA AND JAPAN.

1091 Set of Ancient Chinese "Bullet Money," Fine, very rare, 3 pieces.
1092 Same, variety, (This and preceding lot seem to be alloyed) good, 3 pieces.
1093 1866 Hong Kong, ½ Dollar, uncirculated.
1094 1866 Same, 10 cents, Fine.
1095 1866   "      "     "      good, 2 pieces.
1096 1867   "     20    "    and 5 cents, Fine, 2 pieces.
1097 1868   "     20    "    and two 10 cents, uncirculated, 3 pieces.
1098 1873 Same, 20 cents, and 10 cents, very Fine, 2 pieces.
1099 1874   "      "     "    very Fine.
1100 1874   "     10    "   and 5 cents, uncirculated, 2 pieces.
1101 1874, '5 Same, 10 and 5 cents, uncirculated, 2 pieces.
1102 Japan, One Yen, ($1.00) proof.
1103 Same, Half Yen, uncirculated.
1104   "      uncirculated.
1105   "      Fine.
1106   "      ¼ Yen, uncirculated.
1107   "      10 Sen, (10 cts.), uncirculated.
1108   "      variety, uncirculated.
1109   "      varieties,   "   4 pieces.
1110   "      5 Sen,      "   5   "
1111   "      varieties,   "   5   "
1112   "      uncirculated, 3 pieces.
1113   "      Fine.
1114 Ancient Itzebu, (50 cents,) very Fine, rare.
1115 Same, small, (37 cents,)   "      "      "
1116 Modern Itzebu. (37 cents,) uncirculated.
1117 Same, uncirculated.
1118   "          "     2 pieces.
1119   "          "     2 pieces.
1120   "     2 pieces.
1121   "     ¼ Itzebu, (9¾ cts.) uncirculated, 2 pieces.
1122   "     2 pieces.
1123   "     2 pieces.
1124   "     Fine.

## BRASS AND COPPER COINS OF CHINA, JAPAN, &c.

1125 Large ancient coins, brass, Fine, sizes 21 and 24, 2 pieces.

1126 Same, good to Fine, brass, size 17, 4 pieces.
1127   "    "      "      " size 15, 7 pieces.
1128   "    fair to good,    " size 12, 3 pieces.
1129   "    good, copper, sizes 10 to 12, 3 pieces.
1130   "    large oval coin, 100 P'senny, brass, Fine.
1131   "    4 P'senny, round copper, Fine.
1132   "    brass, Fine.
1133   "    1 P'senny, good to Fine, 5 pieces.
1134   "    copper.
1135   "    set of Modern coins, 2, 1 and ½ Sen, copper.
       uncirculated, 3 pieces.
1136 Same, 1 Sen, uncirculated, 2 pieces.
1137   "    Half Sen, very Fine.
1138 1865 Hong Kong, 1 Cent, brass, good, rare.
1139 1865 Same, "One Mil," very Fine.
1140 1866   "    uncirculated.

## MISCELLANEOUS FOREIGN
## COPPER COINS.

1141 1832 Belgium, 10 and 5 Centimes, fair to good.
     2 pieces.
1142 1833 Same, 5 and 2 Centimes, good, 2 pieces.
1143 1834   "    5 and 2    "    "   3 pieces.
1144 1837   "    5 Centimes, uncirculated.
1145 1841   "    5 and 2 Centimes, good, 2 pieces.
1146 1842   "    5 Centimes, varieties, good, 2 pieces.
1147 1844, '5, '6, '7 Same, 2 Centimes, good to Fine.
     4 pieces.
1148 1848, '9, '56, '9, '61 Same, 5 and 2 Centimes, good to
     Fine, 9 pieces.
1149 1863 Same, Two Centimes, uncirculated.
1150 1870 Same, 10, 5 and 2 Centimes, Fine, 4 pieces
1151 1745, '90 Small Belgium coins, good, 4 pieces.
1152 1738, '49 Russia, 1 Kopek, varieties, good, 2 pieces.
1153 1810, '11 Same, 2 Kopeks, good, 2 pieces.
1154 1811 Same, varieties, good to Fine, 3 pieces.
1155 1812   "      "      "      "   3 pieces.
1156 1813   "      "      "      "   3 pieces.
1157 1814, '18, '20 Same, varieties, good to Fine, 3 pieces.
1158 1834 Same, variety, Fine.
1159 1840   "    1 Kopek, (monogram,) good, 3 pieces.
1160 1841, '2, '4 Same, varieties, good to Fine, 3 pieces.
1161 1851, '8, '9, '60, '2 Same, varieties, Fine, 5 pieces.
1162 1865 Same, "10 Pennia," uncirculated.

1163  1840 Same, ½ Kopek, Fine.
1164  1852, '5, '6 Same, ¼, ½ and 1 Kopek, Fine, 3 pieces.
1165  1857, '62, '3, '5 Same, 1 Kopek, good to Fine,
    4 pieces.
1166  1866 Same, 1 Pennia and 5 Pennia, very Fine, 2 pieces.
1167  1867  "  2 Kopeks, uncirculated, red.
1168  1868  "  1  "  "  "  "
1169  1868, '9, '70, '2 Same, 2 and 1 Kopek, very Fine,
    4 pieces.
1170  Turkey, 10 Gersh, large copper coins, good, 2 pieces.
1171  Same, 5 Gersh, medium size, Fine, 4 pieces.
1172  "  varieties, good to Fine, 5 pieces.
1173  "  small thick coins, varieties, fair to good, 8 pieces
1174  India, large coins, fair to good, varieties, 4 pieces.
1175  Same, small coins, varieties, fair to good, 14 pieces.
1176  1730, '49, '51, '8 Norway, Sweden and Denmark,
    2 and 1 Ore, (arrows,) fair to Fine. 4 pieces.
1177  1759, '6, '1 Same, 1 Ore, good, 3 pieces.
1178  1766 Same, 2 Ore, very thick, Fine.
1179  1771, 1802, '3 Same, ½ and ¼ Skilling, varieties, good
    to Fine, 6 pieces.
1180  1810 Same, 2 Skilling, Fine, 2 pieces.
1181  1814  "  16 Skilling and 1 Skilling, good. 2 pieces
1182  1815, '16 Same, 1 Skilling and ½ Skilling, fair to good
    3 pieces.
1183  1818 Same, 1 Bank Skilling, Fine, 2 pieces.
1184  1819, '20 Same, 1, ½ and ¼ Skillings, (Arms,) good.
    6 pieces.
1185  1822 Same, 2, ½ and ¼ Skilling, thick and thin, fair
    to Fine, 4 pieces.
1186  1828, '9 Same, ¼ Skilling, (arrows,) good, 2 pieces.
1187  1835, '6  "  ⅓, ⅔ and 1 Skilling, Banco, Fine,
    3 pieces.
1188  1839, '40 Same, good to Fine, 3 pieces.
1189  1840, 1 Same, ¼ Skilling, good, 2 pieces.
1190  1842 Same, ⅓, ⅔, 1 and 2 Skilling, good to Fine,
    5 pieces.
1191  1848, '9, '52, '3 Same, ½ and 1 Skilling, Banco, Fine.
    4 pieces.
1192  1856 Same, ½ and 1 Skilling, uncirculated, 2 pieces.
1193  1857, '8 Same, 5 Ore, Fine, 2 pieces.
1194  1860, '3 Same, 1 Skilling, brass, Fine, 2 pieces.
1195  1861, '3  "  5 Ore, Fine, 2 pieces.
1196  1867, '9  "  ½ and 1 Skilling, uncirculated, 2 pieces.
1197  1867, '70  "  ½ and 1  "  very Fine, 3 pieces.

1198 1874, '5 Same, 5 Ore, varieties, uncirculated, 2 pieces.
1199 Same. Selection of large and small pieces, ancient and modern, fair to Fine, 15 pieces.
1200 Miscellaneous assortment of large and small German coins, ancient and modern, good to Fine, 150 pieces.
1201 Same, 60 pieces.
1202 " large coins, good to very Fine, 50 pieces.
1203 " small " mostly Fine, 125 pieces.
1204 " large and small, poor to good, 25 pieces.
1205 Switzerland, large and small, fair to Fine, 65 pieces.

## FOREIGN SILVER COINS &c.

1206 France, 5 Franc, Republic, "Gaule Subalpine," good, rare.
1207 Same, "Union Et Force," pierced, good, scarce.
1208 Same, good, scarce.
1209 1547 Curious German piece, obverse, walled castle, reverse, the man in the moon, good, size 16.
1210 1702, '16 Small Danish coins, fair, 2 pieces.
1211 1720 Louis XV, 2 Francs, good.
1212 1826 Central America, 8 Reals, good.
1213 1842 Same, very Fine.
1214 Republic of Ecuador, 4 Reals, good.
1215 1843 Mexico, 4 Reals, good.
1216 1860 Guatemala, 4 Reals, Fine, pierced.
1217 1876 Repub. of Chili, 1 Peso, Fine.
1218 Siam Bullet Money, set of 3 pieces Fine.
1219 Same, one small piece, with ring attached.
1220 Oriental coins, extremely small, and Fine, 3 pieces.
1221 Germany, large and small coins, ancient and modern, base, fair to good, 27 pieces.
1222 1873 Germany, 20 Pfenning, silver, uncirculated, 2 ps.
1223 1875 Same, 2 pieces.
1224 1874 " 5 Pfenning, base coins, uncirculated, 4 pieces.
1225 1875 Same, 10 Pfenning, base coins, proof, 3 pieces.

## NUMISMATIC AND OTHER PUBLICATIONS.

1226 *Coin Collectors Journal.* Scott & Co,, N. Y. Vols, I, II, III, IV and V to June inc. Complete set 1876 to '80. Subscription for balance of 1880 transferred to purchaser, clean and perfect.

1227 Same, Duplicate numbers, Oct. and Nov. '76, June, Oct Dec. '77, Jan. April, 78, Jan. 80, clean and perfect, 9 pieces.

1228 *Mason's Coin Collectors Herald,* 1879, '80 together with Supplements, (Visitor) 2 vols. Subscription for balance of year transferred to buyer. Clean and perfect.

1229 Numismatic Pilot, La Grange, Ky. Vol 1st; Nos. 1, 2, 3, 4, 1876, '7, clean and perfect.

1230 Same, No. 1, 3, 1876, '77.

1231 Am Journal of Philately, Scott & Co. N. Y. Vol. 1st. 1870 Nos. 1, 2, 3, 4, 5, 7, 8, 9, 10, 11, clean and perfect, 10 pieces.

1232 Curiosity Hunter, Andrus, Rockford, Ill. and Curiosity Collector, Cleveland, Ohio, 1877, odd numbers, clean 11 pieces.

1233 Scott's Coin Advertiser, Boy's Advertiser, Numismatic Journal. Coin and Stamp Journal, Cogan's, Gamp's, Brown's, Mercer's, Stake's, Pierce's, Goerke's, Haseltine and Ahlborn's, Coin and stamp circulars, Jersey Coin Journal, Michigan and St Louis, Philatelist, clean and perfect, 30 pieces.

1234 Visit to the Cabinet of the U. S. Mint, Lippincot & Co., 1876, bound in cloth, 92 pp, new and clean.

1235 Ackerman's Numismatic Manual, Guide to Greek, Roman and English coins, with plates, London 1832 cloth 182 pp, clean and perfect, scarce.

1236 Mathews Coinages of the world, ancient and modern, Scott & Co., N. Y. 1876; copious illustrations, cloth, 305 pp, clean, perfect.

1237 Madden's Jewish Coinage, 254 wood cuts and a plate of alphabets, London 1864, 350 pp, cloth, half roan. gilt top, new and perfect, scarce.

1238 Prime's Coins, Medals and Seals, ancient and modern, Harper Bro's, 1861, profusely illustrated, 292 pp, cloth, clean and perfect.

1239 Eckfeldt & Du Bois' manual of gold and silver coins, of all nations, Phila , 1842, numerous illustrations, 220 pages, cloth, clean and perfect.

1240 Snowden's Washington and National Medals, in the U. S. Mint, with elegant plates, cloth, 203 pages, new and perfect.

1241 Dickeson's Am. Numismatic Manual, Phila , 1865, colored illustrations, with supplementary plates, cloth, 271 pages, clean and perfect. Out of print.

/ '1242 Report of U. S. Mint, 1877, cloth, 109 pages, new and perfect.

1243 Bicknell's Coins of the World, Grover's Manual, Thompson's Coin Chart Manuals, Dye's Gold and Silver Manuals, paper, illustrations, fair to good condition, 5 pieces.

'1244 Harper's Magazine, March 1863. This number contains many illustrations of U, S. and Colonial Coins, &c., scarce.

1245 Coins of the World, Miller, Phila., 1849, colored plates, 74 pages, clean.

1246 Mint Report, 1876, 68 pages, clean.

1247 Same, 1877, 109 pages, clean.

1248 " 1879, 141 " "

'1249 Dead Letter Sale Catalogue, articles accumulated in Dead Letter Office 1877, 83 pages, clean.

1250 Same, 1879, 92 pages, clean.

1251 Catalogue of antiquities, pictures, coins and curiosities, London, 1847, 56 pages, clean.

1252 Catalogue, coins, medals, &c., "For Sale," Haseltine, Phila., 1876, 55 pages, clean, 2 pieces.

1253 Same, 1878, 64 pages, clean.

1254 Mason's Coin Price Catalogue, 1879, '80, 16 pages, clean.

1255 Scott & Co., Illustrations of Copper Coins, 24 pages, clean.

1256 Same, Catalogue of Am. and Foreign coins, 37 pages,

1257 " " Market value of Coins, 38 pages, clean.

1258 Same, Silver and Copper coins, 57 pages, clean.

1259 " U. S. Silver coins, 44 pages, clean.

1260 " Am. and Foreign Silver and Copper coins, 37 pages.

1261 Priced Catalogue of Part I, Bronze Roman and Greek Coins, N. Ponce de Leon, N. Y., 1877, clean.

1262 Same, Part II, Gold and Silver, clean.

1263 Stake's Priced Catalogue, U. S. Coins, 16 pages, clean.

1264 Lusk's U. S. and Foreign Coins, Priced Catalogue, clean, 3 pieces.

1265 Priced Catalogues, Haines' Collection, Part 1 and 2, 1876, 1753 lots, clean.

1266 Same, Cogan, April 12, '77, 949 lots, clean.

1267 Parmelee's Priced Sale Coin Catalogue, June 12, 1876, 2909 lots, clean.

1268  Scott & Co's Stamp Catalogue, illustrated, 46 pages, clean.
1269  Same, Revenue Stamps, 23 pages, clean.
1270   "   U. S. and Foreign Stamps, 46 pages, clean.
1271  Sale Catalogue, Lippman's Collection of Stamps. 16 pages, clean.
1272  London Stamp Collectors' mag., Oct., 1871, clean.
1273  Bestor's Catalogue of coins and medals, Peoria, Ill., 1879, 19 pages, clean.
1274  Catalogues, coin sale, Washington, D. C., 1879, clean. 4 pieces.
1275  Odd numbers of Journal Philately, N. Y., clean. 6 pieces.

## UNPRICED COIN SALE CATALOGUES. &C.

### (ALL CLEAN, NO DUPLICATES.)

1276  1877, '8 Cogan, Haseltine, Scott, Leavitt, 6 pieces.
1277  1877, '8, '9 Chapmans', Cogan, Haseltine, 6 pieces.
1278  1877, '9, '80 Scott, Haines, Chapmans, Cogan, 6 pieces.
1279  1873, '6, '7. '8 Chapmans, Lepere, Haseltine. Cogan, 6 pieces.
1280  1873, '6, '7 Balmanno, Haseltine, Cogan, 6 pieces.
1281  1876, '7, '8 Cogniat, Haseltine, Prosky. Cogan, 6 pieces
1282  1876, '7, '8 Cogan, Haseltine. Harzfeld, 6 pieces.
1283  1876, '7 Prosky, Cogan, Haseltine, Scott, 6 pieces.
1284  1876, '7, '8, '9 Da Silva, Anderson, Stenz, Scott. Cogan, 6 pieces.
1285  1876, '7, '8 Cogan, Haseltine, Scott. 6 pieces
1286  1876, '7, '8 Cogan, Da Silva, Haseltine. Scott, 6 pieces
1287  1877, '8, '9 Haseltine. Scott, Wilder, 6 pieces.
1288  1876, '7, '8 Stenz, Haseltine, Scott, Cogan. 6 pieces.
1289  1877, '8 Leavitt, Haseltine, Cogan, Root. 6 pieces.
1290  1877, '8 Cram, Randall, Cogan, Birch, Scott. 6 pieces
1291  1878 Feb. 6th, Sale Catalogue of over 111,000 Stereoscope Views, (Smith Collection,) Washington. D. C., clean, 2 pieces.
1292  1878 Feb. 18, Japanese Art Treasures, 600 lots. Dowling, Washington, D. C., clean, 3 pieces.
1293  Coin Sale Catalogues, (no covers.) various, 6 pieces.
1294  1864 C. S. A. paper money, $10.00, clean, 50 pieces.
1295  1864 Same, 50 pieces.
1296  1864  "   $20.00, 34 pieces.
1297  1864  "    2.00, 7 pieces.
1298  1864  "    1.00.

1299    Same, small notes, various, 77 pieces.
1300    Southern State Bank Bills, various, clean, 9 pieces.

## THIRD DAY'S SALE.

## MISCELLANEOUS FOREIGN COINS &c.

1301    1850 Switzerland, Helvetia, 20 and 10 Centimes, base, Fine, 2 pieces.
1302    1851 Same, good, 2 pieces.
1303    1858, '9 Same, 20 Centimes, good, 2 pieces.
1304    1872 Same, 10 and 5 Centimes, Fine, 2 pieces.
1305    1877 Brazil, 200 Reis, very large, nickel, Fine.
1306    1874 Chili, 2 Centavos, Republic, nickel, Fine.
1307    1872 Same, ½ Centavo, Fine.
1308    French and German Jetons, large and small, fair to Fine, brass, 6 pieces.
1309    Same, small, 13 pieces.
1310    Spain, old and curious, 17th century, copper and brass, fair, 4 pieces.
1311    Ancient Roman, 1st, 2nd and 3rd, brass, poor, 6 pieces.
1312    1856 Stirling Fishing Club, engraved piece, 2nd prize, silver, size 14.
1313    1863, '6 Hong Kong, 1 Mill, copper, uncirculated. 2 pieces.
1314    Japan, 1 Rin, copper, uncirculated.
1315    Same, "100 P'senny," brass, Fine.
1316    James II, tin piece, uncirculated, rare, size 18.
1317    English Medalets, Royal family, varieties brass, Fine. size 4, 9 pieces.
1318    England, Caroline, Queen Consort of Geo. IV, memorial medal, w. metal, Fine, size 21.
1319    1876 Germany, 10 and 5 Pfennig, nickel, Fine, 2 pieces.
1320    1875 Same, 5 Pfennig, Fine.
1321    1864, '78 Peru, 2 and 1 Centavo, nickel, Fine, 2 pieces.
1322    1822, '3, '8, '31 Buenos Ayres, 1 Decimo, copper, good. 4 pieces.
1323    1827, '30 Same, 20 Reals, National Bank, copper, fair, 4 pieces.
1324    1840, '4, Same, 2, 1 and ½ Reals, copper Fine, 5 pieces.
1325    1853, '4, '5 Same, 2 Reals, Fine, 3 pieces.
1326    1873 Germany, 2 Pfennig, copper, uncirculated, 3 pieces.

1327  1874 Same, 1 Pfennig, uncirculated, 3 pieces.
1328  1859 Danish West Indies, 3 cents, silver, Fine.
1329  1873 Straits Settlements, 5 cents, silver, Fine.
1330  Germany and France, large and small base coins, fair to good, 25 pieces.
1331  Hebrew Shekel, very ancient in appearance, may be genuine. Sold as doubtful, silver, size 15.
1332  Japan, ¼ Bou, gold, (value $1.00) Fine.
1333  American silver medals, medalets, &c., obverse, arms of N. Y. "Presented to N. Y. Regt. of Vol's. in Mexico." reverse, city of Mexico, shipping, &c., tarnished proof, silver, size 32.
1334  Obverse naked bust of Washington, reverse. Presented by Mechanics Institute, Georgetown, D. C. silver, good, size 25.
1335  Obverse bust of Harrison, reverse, "Resolution of Congress, April 4, 1818," silver, pierced, very rare, size 20
1336  Obverse bust of Washington, reverse. Martha, 1792, silver medalet, good, size 13.
1337  1870 Obverse "Pilgrim Jubilee Memorial, 1620" reverse, open Bible. silver plated proof, size 23.
1338  Medalet busts of Washington and Jackson, plain field, silver proof, size 12.
1339  Medalet bust of Washington, reverse, "born, died," &c., silver, good, pierced, size 12.
1340  1864 Medalet, Central Fair, Phila, silver, good, size 12.
1341  Same, pierced, good, 3 pieces.
1342  1876 Medalet Washington and Liberty Bell, silver, proof, pierced, size 12.
1343  Webster Political Token, obv. ship, legend, "Webster Credit Current 1841" reverse, a wrecked ship, legend, "Van Buren, Metallic Current, 1837" silver, proof, excessively rare, perhaps unique, (cost owner $40.00,) size 18.

## UNITED STATES SILVER 20 CENT PIECES, &c.

1344  1875 Proof.
1345  1875 Uncirculated.
1346  1876      "
1347  1876 Very Fine.
1348  1877 Proof, very rare.
1349  1878   "    rare.
1350  1878   "      "

1351  1862 Ten cent piece, proof.
1352  1878  "    "    "    "
1353  1865 Five "    "    "
1354  1867 Silver 3 cent piece, proof, scarce.

## UNITED STATES NICKLE AND BRONZE COINS.

1355  1876 Five cent nickel, proof.
1356  1878  "    "    "    "
1357  1865 Three cent nickel, proof.
1358  1878  "    "    "    "
1359  1864 Two  " piece, uncirculated.
1360  1865  "    "    " proof, scarce.
1361  1866  "    "    " uncirculated.
1362  1867  "    "    "    "
1363  1868  "    "    "    "
1364  1869  "    "    "    "
1365  1870  "    "    "    "
1366  1871  "    "    "    "
1367  1873  "    "    "    "
1368  1856 Nickel cent, dull proof, rare.
1369  1857  "    " uncirculated.
1370  1858  "    " large letters, uncirculated.
1371  1858  "    " small  "    "
1372  1859  "    " uncirculated.
1373  1860  "    "    "
1374  1861  "    "    "
1375  1862  "    "    "
1376  1863  "    "    "
1377  1864  "    " uncirculated.
1378  1864 Bronze  "    "
1379  1865  "    " proof, scarce.
1380  1866  "    " uncirculated.
1381  1867  "    " proof.
1382  1868  "    " uncirculated.
1383  1869  "    "    "
1384  1870, '1, '2, '3, '4 Bronze cents, uncirculated, 5 pieces.
1385  1875, '6, '7, '8, '9  "    "    " 5 pieces.
1386  1876 Bronze cent, proof.

## U. S. SILVER THREE CENT PIECES.

1387  1851 Orleans Mint, uncirculated.
1388  1852 Fine.

1389  1853  Very fine.
1390  1854  Fine.
1391  1855  Good.
1392  1856  Fine.
1393  1857  Good.
1394  1858  Dull proof.
1395  1859  Fine.
1396  1860  "
1397  1861  "
1398  1862  Dull proof.
1399  1863  Proof.
1400  1863  Same.
1401  1864  Proof.
1402  1864  Very fine.
1403  1865  Proof.
1404  1866  Fine.
1405  1867  Proof.
1406  1868  Fine.
1407  1869  "
1408  1870  Very fine.
1409  1871  Proof.
1410  1872  Dull proof.
1411  1873  Proof.

# FOREIGN BRONZE MEDALS, MEDALETS, &C.

1412  1757 Fred'k, King of Prussia, reverse, eagle, legend "Defender of the Protestants," copper, fair, size 24.

1413  Ancient Roman Medal, Minerva, reverse, elephants drawing a triumphal car, fine, rare, size 24.

1414  1769 Shakspeare, "We shall never look upon his like again," reverse, "Jubilee at Stratford," fine, rare, size 21.

1415  King Stephen in armor, reverse, "Born 1135, died 1154," very fine, scarce, size 26.

1416  Prussia, obverse, two medalion busts suspended from an eagle's beak, reverse, 8 medalion busts of distinguished persons, rather indistinct, poor, size 29.

1417  1718 Chas. XII, Spain, reverse, events of his life, in 11 lines, very fine, size 21.

1418  1785 Louis XV, reverse, memorial tablet, fair, size 26.

1419  1789 French medalet, obverse, monument, reverse, attack on the Bastille, fine, size 16.

1420   1805 Napoleon Bonaparte, reverse, cathedral, &c., fair, size 26.

1421   Same, reverse, Badge of Honor, poor, size 26.

1422   1792 French Assignat medal, obverse, soldiers pointing to the Magna Charta, very fine, size 26.

1423   1792 Same, fine.

1424   1792   "   good.

1425   1792   "   fair.

1426   1791   "   fine, size 20, scarce.

1427   1791   "   good, size 20,   "

1428   1820 Angel on a prostrate demon, reverse, woman and child, Spanish, very fine, size 24.

1429   1826 Napoleon Bonaparte, reverse, born, died, &c., very fine, size 26.

1430   1833 Bust of Christian, Denmark, reverse, Angels, nude woman, children, &c., very fine, size 26.

1431   Malhebrun, reverse, wreath, lyre, &c., very fine, size 26

1432   Alex. the Great, Russia, reverse, Angel inscribing the tablet, fine, size 26.

1433   Leopold, Belgium, reverse, female, cornucopia, &c. From the great fire at the Smithsonian Institute, considerably scorched, but all plain, size 32.

1434   Badge, Napoleon Bonaparte, reverse, campaign of 1792 to 1815, very fine, size 20 by 32.

1435   John Alb., mechanic, Prussia, reverse, mechanical emblems, very fine, size 26.

1436   Napoleon full length, reverse, wreath, "Napoleon le Grand," &c., fine, size 16.

1437   1859 Fred. Wm. III, Germany, reverse, interior of a Church, fine, size 28.

1438   Pope Gregory XVI, reverse, male and female figures, fine, size 20.

1439   Count Bismarck, reverse, Strasbourg, Metz, &c., proof, size 20.

1440   Johannes and Eugene, France, reverse, mountains, castles, trees, &c., fine, size 20.

1441   Obverse, two globes, representing Europe and America, reverse, wreath, "Second Epoch," France, good, size 32.

1442   Maximilian, Joseph of Bavaria, reverse, tomb, proof, size 30.

1443   1849 Medalet, commemorating, 1st Ann'y of the French Revolution, dull proof, size 20.

1444   Louis IX, France, reverse, events of his life, electrotype, fine, size 33.

# FOREIGN SILVER COINS.

1445   1708 Spanish Pistareen, Chas. III, good.
1446   1789 ¼ Crown of Austria, good.
1447   1793 Saxony, ⅓ of Thaler, good.
1448   1804 Brunswick, ⅔ of Thaler, fair.
1449   1804 Bank of England Dollar, fine.
1450   1838 Bavaria. 1 Gulden, (35 cts,) fine.
1451   1838 Saxony, " " " good.
1452   1840 Wurtemberg. 1 Gulden, good.
1453   1840 Bremen, 36 Grote, fine.
1454   1841 Baden, 1 Gulden, good.
1455   1842 Same, good.
1456   1846 Bremen, 36 Grote.
1457   1847 Wurtemberg, 2 Gulden, fine.
1458   1848 Saxony Thaler, very fine
1459   1848 Bavaria, 1 Gulden, good.
1460   1854 Saxony, Thaler, fine.
1461   1856 Same, fine.
1462   1858 Austria, Thaler, damaged proof.
1463   1859 Prussia, Thaler, fine.
1464   1859 Portugal, 500 Reis, fine.
1465   1860 Frankfurt, Thaler, uncirculated.
1466   1860 Prussia, Thaler, uncirculated.
1467   1861 Austria, " "
1468   1861 Frankfurt, 2 Thaler piece, very fine.
1469   1861 Baden Thaler, uncirculated.
1470   1864 Saxony " very Fine.
1471   1865 Austria, 1 Florin, very Fine.
1472   1866 Netherlands, 1 Gulden, very Fine.
1473   1872 Austria, 1 Florin, uncirculated.
1474   1874 Straits Settlements, (set) 20, 10 and 5 cts. uncirculated, 3 pieces.
1475   1874 Same, 3 pieces.
1476   1874 Same, 5 cents.
1477   Large German coins, not wholly silver, varieties, Fair to Fine, 13 pieces.

## WASHINGTON BRONZE & COPPER
### PIECES, &C.

1478   1783 Unity Cent, brass, very Fine, scarce.
1479   1791 Large Eagle Cent, copper, fair, gilt, rare.
1480   1791 Small " " electrotype, Fine.
1481   1792 Electrotype copy of W. Half Dollar, Fine,

1482   1792 Same, struck copy (Idler's) copper, proof.
1483   Bust, legend, "Geo. Washington, Born, Died, &c." rev.
      late President of the U. S. of A. copper, good, rare,
      size 24.
1484   1795 Grate Cent, very Fine, rare.
1485   Medalet, bust by Key, rev., "Providence left him child-
      less." copper, proof, size 18.
1486   1797 Presidency relinquished, copper, good, size 29.
1487   1797 Same, bronze proof, size 26.
1488   Bust, reverse " With Courage and Fidelity," &c., copper,
      fair, rare, size 26.
1489   " Double Headed" Cent, Fine, scarce.
1490   Liberty and Security piece, electrotype, Fine.
1491   1783 Unity Cent, brass, fair.
1492   Bust, Born, Died, &c , thick, proof, bronze, size 20.
1493   Same, reverse, "The Union is the Main Prop of our
      Liberty," proof, size 16.
1494   Same, reverse, "Time Increases His Fame," thick,
      proof, size 18.
1495   Same, thin, proof.
1496   Memorial medalet, bronze, proof, size 14.
1497   Same, very fine.
1498   Bust, reverse, Dickeson's card, copper, proof, size 20.
1499   Washington's Headquarters at Tappan, reverse, Liberty
      Tree, copper, proof, size 20.
1500   Bust surrounded by 13 stars, reverse, Headquarters at
      White Plains, copper, proof, size 18.
1501   Same,  Headquarters near Chad's Ford.
1502      "     Valley Forge.
1503      "     Morristown.
1504      "     Harlem.
1505      "     White Marsh.
1506      "     Tappan, N. Y.
1507      "     Sufferns,  "
1508      "     Harlem,  "
1509      "     Newburg,  "
1510   Mint Cabinet Medal, bronze proof, size 38.
1511   Same, copper, dull proof.
1512   Mint Medalet, Pollock, thick, bronze proof, size 20.
1513   Same, thin bronze proof.
1514   Sanitary Fair, Phila., copper, fine, size 12, 2 pieces.
1515   1869 Norwalk, Conn. memorial medal, bronze proof,
      size 24.
1516   Memorial medalet, "He is in Glory, and the World in
      Tears," w. metal, pierced, good, rare, size 18.

'1517   1859 Bust, reverse, Cogan's Card, w. metal, proof, size 20.
"1518   1861 Bust surrounded by eagle, stars, flags, &c., reverse, equestrian monument, Union Sq., N. Y., w. metal, silvered, scarce, size 32.
'1519   1869 Norwalk, Conn. memorial medal, w. metal, proof, size 24.
1520   1876 Bust, reverse, signing the Declaration, w. metal proof, size 26.
"1521   1876 Bust, reverse, Washington Monument, w. metal, proof, size 25.
1522   1876 Same, Independence Hall, proof, size 24.
"1523   1876   "   reverse, Liberty Bell, proof, size 24.
'1524   1876   "   "   "Reward of Merit," proof, size 24.
1525   1876 Bust, reverse, "Free and U. S.," w. metal, proof, size 24.
       (Lots 1521 to 1525 inc. are from the Wood series)
.1526   Bust, reverse, Independence Hall, w. metal, proof, size 24.
"1527   Bust, reverse, Mount Vernon, w. metal, proof, size 22.
"1528   Bust, reverse, Born, Died, &c., w. metal, proof, size 20.
'1529   Bust, reverse, "Dedicated to the Children of America," w. metal, proof, size 22.
"1530   Bust, reverse, Battle of Trenton, w. metal, proof, size 22.

## UNITED STATES CENTS.

.1531   1793 wreath, twig inclines to the right, good, rare.
'1532   1793 chain, pierced, very poor.
'1533   1793 lettered edge, wreath, extremely poor.
1534   1793 Same, poorer than preceding, 2 pieces.
1535   1794 fallen 4, nearly fine, dark.
1536   1794 broad close date, nearly fine, dark.
1537   1794 good, varieties, 3 pieces.
1538   1794 large and small planchet, fair, 2 pieces.
1539   1795 One Cent, high in wreath, good.
1540   1795 Same, poor, 2 pieces.
1541   .1796 Liberty Cap, good.
.1542   1796 Fillet Head, poor in date.
'1543   1797 small planchet, fine, dark.
1544   1797 large planchet, indented edge, good.
1545   1797 Same, small planchet, indented edge, good.
1546   1797 large broad date,   "   "   "
1547   1797 fair to good, varieties, 3 pieces.
'1548   1798 large 8, nearly fine.

| | |
|---|---|
| 1549 | 1798 Same, small 8, nearly fine, 2 pieces. |
| 1550 | 1798 good, varieties, 10 pieces. |
| 1551 | 1798 Same, fair, 6 pieces. |
| 1552 | 1799 over '98, fair, rare. |
| 1553 | 1799 altered dates, very poor, 2 pieces. |
| 1554 | 1800 over '99, nearly fine, black. |
| 1555 | 1800 Same, good. |
| 1556 | 1800 perfect date, varieties, good, 3 pieces. |
| 1557 | 1801, ₀₀₀, nearly fine. |
| 1558 | 1801, ₁₀₀ over ₀₀₀ nearly fine. |
| 1559 | 1801 Same, broken die, very good. |
| 1560 | 1801 double portrait, poor. |
| 1561 | 1801 varieties, fair, 3 pieces. |
| 1562 | 1802 ₀₀₀, fine, 2 pieces. |
| 1563 | 1802 ₀₀₀, good, 2 pieces. |
| 1564 | 1802 Varieties, good, 3 pieces. |
| 1565 | 1803 Large ₁₀₀, fine, dark, 2 pieces. |
| 1566 | 1803 Small ₁₀₀,  "    "  2 pieces. |
| 1567 | 1803 Few varieties, all good, 8 pieces. |
| 1568 | 1805 Good, 4 pieces. |
| 1569 | 1805 Fair, pierced. |
| 1570 | 1806 Poor. |
| 1571 | 1807 over '6, good, 4 pieces. |
| 1572 | 1807 Fair to good, 3 pieces. |
| 1573 | 1808 Good, 2 pieces. |
| 1574 | 1809 Poor, 2 pieces. |
| 1575 | 1810 Nearly fine, varieties, 5 pieces. |
| 1576 | 1810 Varieties, good, 8 pieces. |
| 1577 | 1811 Poor, 2 pieces. |
| 1578 | 1812 Good, 4 pieces. |
| 1579 | 1813 Poor. |
| 1580 | 1814 Crossed 4 and plain 4, good, 2 pieces. |
| 1581 | 1816 Good. |
| 1582 | 1817 Nearly fine, black. |
| 1583 | 1817—15 stars, good. |
| 1584 | 1817 Varieties, good, 3 pieces. |
| 1585 | 1818 Nearly fine. |
| 1586 | 1819 Large and small date, fine, 2 pieces. |
| 1587 | 1819 Good, 5 pieces. |
| 1588 | 1820 Large and small 0, nearly fine, 2 pieces. |
| 1589 | 1820 Some varieties, good, 9 pieces. |
| 1590 | 1821 Good, 2 pieces. |
| 1591 | 1822   " |
| 1592 | 1823   "   3 pieces. |
| 1593 | 1824   "   varieties, 2 pieces. |

1591  1825  Fair.
1595  1826  Nearly fine, black, 4 pieces.
1596  1826  Good, 2 pieces.
1597  1827  Nearly fine.
1598  1827  Good, 3 pieces.
1599  1828  Very good, 2 pieces.
1600  1828  Good, 5 pieces.
1601  1829  Nearly fine, black, 4 pieces.
1602  1829  Very good, 4 pieces.
1603  1830  Very good, 3 pieces.
1604  1831  Nearly fine, varieties, black, 2 pieces.
1605  1831  Very good, 2 pieces.
1606  1832  Nearly fine, 3 pieces.
1607  1832  Good, 5 pieces.
1608  1833  Nearly fine, 2 pieces.
1609  1834  Same, 4 pieces.
1610  1834  Fine, 2 pieces.
1611  1834  Very good, 3 pieces.
1612  1835  Nearly fine, 2 pieces.
1613  1835  Good, 4 pieces.
1614  1836  Nearly fine, black.
1615  1837  Fine, 5 pieces.
1616  1837  Very good, 7 pieces.
1617  1838  Fine, 4 pieces.
1618  1839  Booby Head, very good.
1619  1839, '38. Head, nearly fine.
1620  1839, '40 Head, fine, 4 pieces.
1621  1839, '38 Head, good, 2 pieces.
1622  1839  Booby Head, good.
1623  1840  Nearly fine, 2 pieces.
1624  1841    "        "
1625  1842  Large and Small date, very good, 2 pieces.
1626  1843  Small letters, fine, 2 pieces.
1627  1843  Large    "      very good, 4 pieces.
1628  1844  Large and Small date, very good, 2 pieces.
1629  1845  Fine, 2 pieces.
1630  1846    "    dark, varieties, 2 pieces.
1631  1847    "    2 pieces.
1632  1848  Very fine, 2 pieces.
1633  1849, '50  Fine, 2 pieces.
1634  1850, '2, '3  Very good, 5 pieces.
1635  1855  Straight and slanting date, nearly fine, 2 pieces.
1636  1856  Very fine, 4 pieces.
1637  1857  Large date, very fine, 3 pieces.
1638  1857    "        "    fine, 2 pieces.

1639    1857 Large date, good, 3 pieces.
1640    1793, '4, '5, '7, '8, 1800, '1, '2, '3, '5, '7, '8, '10, '12, '14,
        '17, '18, '19, '20, '21, '3, '4, '5, '6, '8, '9, '30, '1, '2, '4,
        '5, '6, '7, '8, '40, '2, '6, '8, '56, '57, poor to fine, mostly
        old dates, 81 pieces.

## UNITED STATES HALF CENTS.

1641    1793 Black and rusty, very little circulated, rare.
1642    1794 Very good, scarce, 4 pieces.
1643    1795 Thick planchet, lettered edge, good, scarce.
1644    1795 Thin Planchet, good.
1645    1795 Same, poor, 2 pieces.
1646    1797 Good, 2 pieces.
1647    1800 Nearly fine, 2 pieces.
1648    1802 Very good, rare.
1649    1802 Same, good.
1650    1803 Very good, 3 pieces.
1651    1804 Fine, varieties, 4 pieces.
1652    1804 Good,    "     3 pieces.
1653    1805 Nearly fine.
1654    1806 Very fine, light olive, 2 pieces.
1655    1807 Very good.
1656    1808 Fine, 2 pieces.
1657    1808 Very good, 3 pieces.
1658    1809 Very fine, 5 pieces.
1659    1810    "     "     scarce.
1660    1810    "    good.
1661    1811 Broken Die, nearly fine, rare.
1662    1811 Good, black, 2 pieces.
1663    1825 Fine, 3 pieces.
1664    1826 Very fine, 2 pieces.
1665    1828 Uncirculated.
1666    1828 Very fine.
1667    1828 12 stars, fine, 2 pieces.
1668    1829 Fine, 2 pieces.
1669    1832    "    2 pieces.
1670    1833 Very fine, 2 pieces.
1671    1834 Very fine, 2 pieces.
1672    1835 Uncirculated, 2 pieces.
1673    1849 Fine, 2 pieces.
1674    1850 Very fine, 2 pieces.
1675    1851 Fine, 2 pieces.
1676    1853    "    2 pieces.
1677    1854 Very fine, 2 pieces.

1678 1855 Fine, 2 pieces.
1679 1856 Very fine, scarce.
1680 1857 Uncirculated, red, scarce.
1681 Lot of half cents, mostly old dates, poor to fine, 52 pieces.

## FOREIGN SILVER MEDALS, MEDALETS, COINS, &C.

1682 German medal, by Loos; obverse, wreath of roses en-
twined around two torches; legend, "*Sonne Du Siehst
Ein Gluecklliches Paar;*" reverse,. one of the Muses,
very fine, size 24.
1683 Medal, St. George and the dragon, legend, "St. George
the Martyr," reverse, Saviour bearing the cross, very
fine and beautifully milled, thick, rare, size 20.
1684 Republic of Berne; obverse, shield, crown, bear in the
centre, reverse, mechanic resting on one knee, tools,
&c., very fine, beautifully milled, engrailed edge,
rare, size 20.
1685 Same, Goddess of Liberty seated by a rostrum, Cupid,
cornucopia, &c., reverse, "*Invitat Prettis Animos;*"
fine, rare, size 16.
1686 1818 Russia, ½ Rouble, good.
1687 Germany, Leopold, ½ Florin, good.
1688 Medalet, obverse, tomb, globe, &c., reverse, scales, fine,
size 13.
1689 1859 Danish W. Indies, 5 cts, (ship,) fine.
1690 1816 Same, "X Shilling," good, 2 pieces.
1691 1842 Prussia, ½ Thaler, fine.
1692 1861 Same, overlapped busts of William and Augusta,
reverse, eagle, crowns, &c., very fine, scarce.
1693 1863 Bremen, obverse, arms, "Ein Thaler Gold," reverse, wreath, "Zur 50 Jæhrigen Jubelfeier, &c.," silver, proof, size 21
1694 1868 Austria, 20 Pfennig, uncirculated.

## FOREIGN WHITE METAL MEDALS, &C.

1695 Pope Innocence XI, reverse, female figure, fine, varnished, size 24.
1696 Richard II, reverse, tomb, electrotype, size 26.
1697 Henry II, reverse, tomb, size 26.
1698 France, obverse, nude man standing, reverse, ship, fine,
varnished, 2 pieces, size 21.

1799  Joseph and Maria Theresa, incused, fine, size 32.
1700  Fred II, Prussia, incused, fine, size 26.
1701  German medal representing a flood in the North of Europe, Feb. 27, 1784; very fine size 29.
1702  1803 Barber Beaumont, reverse, "Duke of Cumberland's Sharp Shooters," fair, size 26.
1703  Napoleon by Andrieu, reverse, blank, very fine, size 42.
1704  Same, reverse, Badge of Honor, good, varnished, size 26.
1705  "      "    nude male figure, varnished, good, size 26.
1706  Same, reverse, blank, cast, good, size 26.
1707  Louis of France, reverse, globe, sun, &c., very fine, size 24.
1708  1806 Wurtemberg, Fred V, reverse, a crown, damaged proof, size 29.
1709  France, Soldier, monument, flags, &c., reverse, "Brave Defenders," &c., cast, fine, size 26.
1710  1814 Wurtemberg, Fred. Wm., reverse. 3 flags, proof, size 23.
1711  1842 Same, ruins of a castle, reverse, German Cathedral, electrotype, fine, size 28.
1712  1845 Brunel, reverse, Thames Tunnel, dull proof, size 24.
1713  1353 Dargan, reverse, Dublin Exposition, proof, size 28.
1714  Humboldt, reverse, "Earth and Heaven He explored," &c., proof, size 32.
1715  Same, silvered, dull proof.
1716  1859 Burns, reverse, "Centenary of Birth," &c., pierced, fine, size 26.
1717  1863 Obverse, battle (Germany and France 1813,) proof, size 26.
1718  1867 Napoleon III, reverse, Paris Exposition, gilt, fine, size 32.
1719  Rome, bust of a Cardinal; reverse, Cardinal's hat, shield, &c., proof, size 30.
1720  Father Mathew, front face, reverse, "Pledge," proof, size 21.
1721  Tin shells, with busts, medalets, &c., poor to fine, 6 pieces.

## UNITED STATES NICKEL AND BRONZE COINS.

1722  1864, '9 Two ct. pieces, uncirculated, 2 pieces.
1723  1872 Same, dull proof, scarce.

1724 1856 Nickel cent, Fine, rare.
1725 1857, '8 uncirculated, 2 pieces.
1726 1858, '9, '60, '1 Same, uncirculated, 4 pieces.
1727 1862, '3, '4 " " 3 pieces.
1728 1864, '5, '6, '7, '8, '9 Same, uncirculated, 7 pieces.
1729 1870, '1, '2, '3, '4 " " 5 pieces.
1730 1875, '7, '8, '9, '80 Same, uncirculated, 5 pieces.

## AMERICAN COLONIAL COINS.

1731 1785 Conn. Cent, fair, scarce.
1732 1786 Same, varieties, fair, 3 pieces
1733 1787 " Auctopi, fair, scarce, 2 pieces.
1734 1787 " Inde Et Lir, fair to good, varieties, scarce, 4 pieces.
1735 1787 Same, last 7 very distant from 8, poor, rare.
1736 1787 " "Horned Bust," good, scarce.
1737 1787 " Connec., letters very much separated, good, rare.
1738 1787 Same, Connect., poor, rare.
1739 1787 " Connec., last C far below its proper place, fair, rare.
1740 1787 Same, varieties, good to Fine, 5 pieces.
1741 1787 " " " 10 pieces,
1742 1787 " "Au Au Econnec," double bust, double strike, obverse, good, reverse, poor.
1743 1787 Same, varieties, poor, 14 pieces.
1744 1788 " Georgius Rex, reverse, Inde Et Lib., fair, rare.
1745 1788 Same, varieties, fair, 5 pieces.
1746 1701 N. Jersey Cent, altered from 1787, very good.
1747 1786 Same, brass alloy, small planchet, scarce.
1748 1786 " good.
1749 1787 N. J., small planchet, small plow, naked horse head, very good, scarce.
1750 1787 Same, large plow, broad date, good.
1751 1787 " small plow, small close date, good.
1752 1787 " varieties, fair to good, 9 pieces.
1753 1788 " large planchet, good, slightly corroded.
1754 1773 Virginia large planchet, fine, scarce.
1755 1773 Same, small planchet, good.
1756 1723 Wood ½ Penny, good, scarce.
1757 1787 Immunis Columbia, electrotype.
1758 1787 Same, thin solid copper, Fine.
1759 U. S. A. Bar cent, electrotype.
1760 N. Carolina brass piece, fine.

## FACETIOUS PIECES.

1761 Remarkable ancient Roman medal. Bust of Pricapus; rev., very curious example of the ingenuity of the Romans in *facetia*. Original, Fine, size 28.

1762 Solid copper Hindoo Idol, nude, very ancient looking, and certainly curious; about 2½ inches from top to bottom; (in a sitting position) good.

1763 French example of *facetia*. Medal with blank reverse. Ob. a lesson in therapenties; copper, fine, size 18.

1764 Copper cast; two nude Figures, size 24.

1765 German brass Jeton. "The Beginning and the End;" brass, nearly fine, size 16.

## MISCELLANEOUS BOOKS, COINS, MEDALS, &C.

1766 Set of large Centennial Medals, various, black walnut, in box, 6 pieces.

1767 "U. S. Naval Astronomical Expedition to the Southern Hemisphere, 1849, '50, '1, '2," copious plates and maps, (Cities, Towns, &c.,) Vol. I. large quarto, half calf, 556 pages, clean and perfect, scarce.

1768 Same, Vol. II, colored plates of beasts, birds, fishes and reptiles, 300 pages, mostly illustrations, scarce.

1769 Busts of Napoleon and Engenie, reverse, "Napoleon III Empereur" &c., proof, brass, in morocco velvet lined case, size 32.

1770 Bust of Lafayette, reverse, "The Defender" &c., bronze proof, size 30.

1771 8 Medalion busts of Presidents, Washington to Van Buren, proof, w. metal, silvered, size 30.

1772 1875 Haverford College, Pa. reverse, "For Under Graduate Oration," bronze, very fine, size 26.

1773 Washington, reverse, Independence Hall, w. metal, very fine, size 24.

1774 Harrison, reverse, "Log Cabin," w. metal, Fine, pierced, size 21.

1775 1791, '3 Washington cent and U. S. ½ cent, lead, good, 2 pieces.

1776 Liberty, reverse, U. S. A., 3 cents, electrotype, size 16

1777 1868 Seymour and Blair, thick, brass, Fine, size 18.

1778 1868 " rev. " w. metal, Fine, size 16.

1779 1868 Same, reverse, star, Fine, size 16.

1780  1870 Gen. Grant, thick, Fine, size 17
1781  1876 Greely, reverse, "For President," w. metal, good, size 16.
1782  Lincoln, reverse, Wide-a-Wakes, proof, size 12.
1783  Politicals, lead and w. metal, various, poor, 5 pieces.
1784  1837 "Half Cent Worth of Pure Copper," very Fine, scarce.
1785  1837 Same, uncirculated.
1786  U. S. nickel cents, mis-struck, Fine, 4 pieces.
1787  1837 Feuchtwanger cent, nickel, Fine.
1788  1783 Washington cent, "Unity," brass, good.
1789  1801 Roman Baiocco, copper, large and small, very Fine, 2 pieces.
1790  1813 Small Java coin, curious, Fine.
1791  1820 Same, varieties, Fine, 4 pieces.
1792  1661 Small ancient German coin, Fine.
1793  Col. Kirk, reverse, "Britons Happy Isle," copper, Fine, scarce.
1794  Roman, Claudius II, brass, fair.
1795  1750 George III, Burlesque Pieces, copper, good, 5 pieces.
1796  Louis XVI, reverse, "Music Charms," varieties, copper, Fine, 2 pieces.
1797  Japan, 1 Sen and $\frac{1}{2}$ Sen, copper, Fine, 2 pieces.
1798  1693 Wm. and Mary Half Penny, poor, scarce.
1799  1681 Curious old Spanish coin, copper, Fine.
1800  Hayty. 25 cents, and 12 cents, base, fine, 3 pieces.
1801  1721, Duke of Cumberland, rev. "Rebellion justly rewarded," Carlisle, Dec. 1745, copper, fine, size 22.
1802  1876 Centennial Medal, by authority of Congress, brass, gilt, very fine, size 24.
1803  1838 " Am I not a Woman and a Sister ?" good to fine, 4 pieces.
1804  1877 Medalet struck in Philadelphia Exhibition, copper, Fine, size 16, 2 pieces.
1805  U. S. Arsenal, Springfield, Mass., copper, proof, size 18.
1806  1869 Bolen, rev. " Die Sinker, &c." copper, proof, size 16.
1807  Robbins, Royce & Co., N. Y., card, nickel, proof, scarce, size 12, 2 pieces.
1808  Washington, rev. Martha, copper, fine, size 13.
1809  Am. political medalets, all different, brass and copper, good to fine, 16 pieces.
1810  Scripture medalets with verses, copper, fine, size 18, 2 pieces.

1811  Brass cards, coins, medalets, &c., good to fine, various, 22 pieces.
1812  Hayti, 25 cts. varieties, brass. fine, 3 pieces.
1813  Large thick foreign coins, medals, &c , copper and brass. poor to fine, 17 pieces.
1814  Same, medium size, copper, 118 pieces.
1815  Roman coin, Empress of Solonia, bust on each side, (with MS. description,) 3d brass, fine, rare.
1816  Same, Lucullus, (with MS. description,) good, rare.
1817  Small Foreign and American coins, tokens and medalets, copper, brass and nickel, poor to fine, 83 pieces.
1818  Lot mis-struck copper cents and other curious pieces, poor, 8 pieces.

www.ingramcontent.com/pod-product-compliance
Lightning Source LLC
Chambersburg PA
CBHW021540270326
41930CB00008B/1321